NSA Encryption Devices
Encryption Systems of the National Security Agency

Contents

Chapter 1

NSA encryption systems

The National Security Agency took over responsibility for all U.S. Government encryption systems when it was formed in 1952. The technical details of most NSA-approved systems are still classified, but much more about its early systems have become known and its most modern systems share at least some features with commercial products.

Rotor machines from the 1940s and 1950s were mechanical marvels. The first generation electronic systems were quirky devices with cantankerous punched card readers for loading keys and failure-prone, tricky-to-maintain vacuum tube circuitry. Late 20th century systems are just black boxes, often literally. In fact they are called *blackers* in NSA parlance because they convert plaintext classified signals (*red*) into encrypted unclassified ciphertext signals (*black*). They typically have electrical connectors for the red signals, the black signals, electrical power, and a port for loading keys. Controls can be limited to selecting between key fill, normal operation, and diagnostic modes and an all important *zeroize* button that erases classified information including keys and perhaps the encryption algorithms. 21st century systems often contain all the sensitive cryptographic functions on a single, tamper-resistant integrated circuit that supports multiple algorithms and allows over-the-air or network re keying, so that a single hand-held field radio can interoperate with most current NSA cryptosystems. AN/PRC-152

1.1 Security factors

NSA has to deal with many factors in ensuring the security of communication and information (COMSEC and INFOSEC in NSA jargon):

- *Confidentiality* and *authentication* - making sure messages cannot be read by unauthorized people and that they cannot be forged (nonrepudiation). Little is publicly known about the algorithms NSA has developed for protecting classified information, what NSA calls Type 1 algorithms. In 2003, for the first time in its history, NSA approved two published algorithms, Skipjack and AES for Type 1 use in NSA approved systems.

- *Traffic flow security* - making sure an adversary cannot obtain information from traffic analysis, often accomplished by link encryption.

- *Key management* - getting keys securely to thousands of crypto boxes in the field, perhaps the most challenging part of any encryption system. One NSA goal is benign fill (technology for distributing keys in a way that the humans never have access to plaintext key).

- *Investigative access* - making sure encrypted communications are accessible to the U.S. Government. While few would argue with the need for the government to access its own internal communications, the NSA Clipper chip proposal to extend this key escrow requirement to public use of cryptography was highly controversial.

- *TEMPEST* - protecting plaintext from compromise by electronic, acoustic or other emanations.

- *Tamper resistance, tamper-evident, self-destruct* - ensuring security even if encryption systems are physically accessed without authorization or are captured.

- Meeting military specifications for size, weight, power consumption, MTBF and ruggedness to fit in mobile platforms.

- *Electromagnetic pulse hardening* - protecting against nuclear explosion effects, particularly electromagnetic pulse.

- Ensuring compatibility with military and commercial communication standards.

- Controlling cost - making sure encryption is affordable so units that need it have it. There are many costs beyond the initial purchase price, including the manpower to operate and maintain the systems and to ensure their security and the cost of key distribution.

- Enabling secure communication with NATO, allied and coalition forces without compromising secret methods.

1.2   Five generations of NSA encryption

The large number of encryption systems that NSA has developed in its half century of operation can be grouped into five generations (decades given are very approximate):

1.2.1   First generation: electromechanical

KL-7 at NSA Museum.

First generation NSA systems were introduced in the 1950s and were built on the legacy of NSA's World War II predecessors and used rotor machines derived from the SIGABA design for most high level encryption; for example, the KL-7. Key distribution involved distribution of paper key lists that described the rotor arrangements, to be changed each day (the *cryptoperiod*) at midnight, GMT. The highest level traffic was sent using one-time tape systems, including the British 5-UCO, that required vast amounts of paper tape keying material.

1.2.2   Second generation: vacuum tubes

An array of KW-26 encryption systems.

Second generation systems (1970s) were all electronic designs based on vacuum tubes and transformer logic. Algorithms appear to be based on linear feedback shift registers, perhaps with some non-linear elements thrown in to make them more difficult to cryptanalyze. Keys were loaded by placing a punched card in a locked reader on the front panel.[1] The cryptoperiod was still usually one day. These systems were introduced in the late 1960s and stayed in use until the mid-1980s. They required a great deal of care and maintenance, but were not vulnerable to EMP. The discovery of the Walker spy ring provided an impetus for their retirement, along with remaining first generation systems.

1.2.3   Third generation: integrated circuits

Third generation systems (1980s) were transistorized and based on integrated circuits and likely used stronger algorithms. They were smaller and more reliable. Field maintenance was often limited to running a diagnostic mode and replacing a

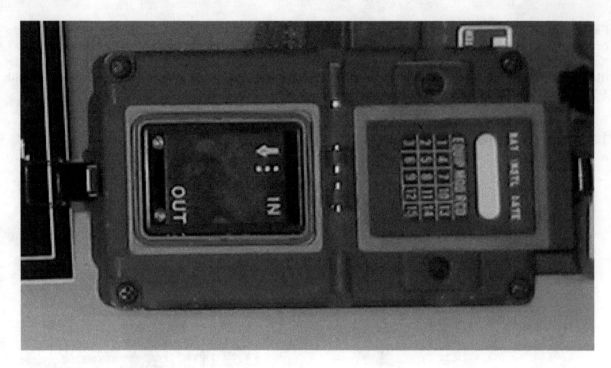

KOI-18 field paper tape reader.

complete bad unit with a spare, the defective box being sent to a depot for repair. Keys were loaded through a connector on the front panel. NSA adopted the same type of connector that the military used for field radio handsets as its fill connector. Keys were initially distributed as strips of punched paper tape that could be pulled through a hand held reader (KOI-18) connected to the fill port. Other, portable electronic fill devices (KYK-13, etc.) were available as well.

1.2.4   Fourth generation: electronic key distribution

STU-III phones with crypto-ignition keys.

Fourth generation systems (1990s) use more commercial packaging and electronic key distribution. Integrated circuit technology allowed backward compatibility with third generation systems. Security tokens, such as the KSD-64 crypto ignition key (**CIK**) were introduced. Secret splitting technology allows encryptors and CIKs to be treated as unclassified when they were separated. Later the Fortezza card, originally introduced as part of the controversial Clipper chip proposal, were employed as tokens. Cryptoperiods were much longer, at least as far as the user was concerned. Users of secure telephones like the STU-III only have to call a special phone number once a year to have their encryption updated. Public key methods (FIREFLY) were introduced for electronic key management (EKMS). Keys can now be generated by individual commands instead of coming from NSA by courier. A common handheld fill device (the AN/CYZ-10) was introduced to replace the plethora of devices used to load keys on the many third generation systems that were still widely used. Encryption support was provided for commercial standards such as Ethernet, IP (originally developed by DOD's ARPA), and optical fiber multiplexing. Classified networks, such as SIPRNet (Secret Internet Protocol Router Network) and JWICS (Joint Worldwide Intelligence Communications System), were built using commercial Internet technology with secure communications links between "enclaves" where classified data was processed. Care had to be taken to ensure that there were no insecure connections between the classified networks and the public Internet.

1.2.5 Fifth generation: network-centric systems

In the twenty-first century, communication is increasingly based on computer networking. Encryption is just one aspect of protecting sensitive information on such systems, and far from the most challenging aspect. NSA's role will increasingly be to provide guidance to commercial firms designing systems for government use. HAIPE solutions are examples of this type of product (e.g., KG-245A and KG-250). Other agencies, particularly NIST, have taken on the role of supporting security for commercial and sensitive but unclassified applications. NSA's certification of the unclassified NIST-selected AES algorithm for classified use "in NSA approved systems" suggests that, in the future, NSA may use more non-classified algorithms. The KG-245A and KG-250 use both classified and unclassified algorithms. The NSA Information Assurance Directorate is leading the Department of Defense Cryptographic Modernization Program, an effort to transform and modernize Information Assurance capabilities for the 21st century. It has three phases:

- Replacement- All at risk devices to be replaced.

- Modernization- Integrate modular programmable/embedded crypto solutions.

- Transformation- Be compliant to Global Information Grid/NetCentric requirements.

NSA has helped develop several major standards for secure communication: the *Future Narrow Band Digital Terminal (FNBDT)* for voice communications, *High Assurance Internet Protocol Interoperability Encryption- Interoperability Specification (HAIPE)* for computer networking and Suite B encryption algorithms.

1.3 NSA encryption by type of application

The large number of encryption systems that NSA has developed can be grouped by application:

1.3.1 Record traffic encryption

During World War II, written messages (known as **record traffic**) were encrypted off line on special, and highly secret, rotor machines and then transmitted in five letter code groups using Morse code or teletypewriter circuits, to be decrypted off-line by similar machines at the other end. The SIGABA rotor machine, developed during this era continued to be used until the mid-1950s, when it was replaced by the KL-7, which had more rotors.

The KW-26 ROMULUS was a second generation encryption system in wide use that could be inserted into teletypewriter circuits so traffic was encrypted and decrypted automatically. It used electronic shift registers instead of rotors and became very popular (for a COMSEC device of its era), with over 14,000 units produced. It was replaced in the 1980s by the more compact KG-84, which in turn was superseded by the KG-84-interoperable KIV-7.

1.3.2   Fleet broadcast

U.S. Navy ships traditionally avoid using their radios to prevent adversaries from locating them by direction finding. The Navy also needs to maintain traffic security, so it has radio stations constantly broadcasting a stream of coded messages. During and after World War II, Navy ships copied these *fleet broadcasts* and used specialized *call sign encryption* devices to figure out which messages were intended for them. The messages would then be decoded off line using SIGABA or KL-7 equipment.

The second generation KW-37 automated monitoring of the fleet broadcast by connecting in line between the radio receiver and a teleprinter. It, in turn, was replaced by the more compact and reliable third generation KW-46.

1.3.3   Strategic forces

NSA has the responsibility to protect the command and control systems for nuclear forces. The KG-3X series is used in the U.S. government's *Minimum Essential Emergency Communications Network* and the *Fixed Submarine Broadcast System* used for transmission of emergency action messages for nuclear and national command and control of U.S. strategic forces. The Navy is replacing the KG-38 used in nuclear submarines with KOV-17 circuit modules incorporated in new long-wave receivers, based on commercial VME packaging. In 2004, the U.S. Air Force awarded contracts for the initial system development and demonstration (SDD) phase of a program to update these legacy generation systems used on aircraft.

1.3.4   Trunk encryption

Modern communication systems multiplex many signals into wideband data streams that are transmitted over optical fiber, coaxial cable, microwave relay, and communication satellites. These wide-band circuits require very fast encryption systems.

The WALBURN family (KG-81, KG-94/194, KG-94A/194A, KG-95) of equipment consists of high-speed bulk encryption devices used primarily for microwave trunks, high-speed land-line circuits, video teleconferencing, and T-1 satellite channels. Another example is the KG-189, which support SONET optical standards up to 2.5 Gbit/s.

Digital Data encryptors such as KG-84 family which includes the TSEC/KG-84, TSEC/KG-84A and TSEC/KG-82, TSEC/KG-84A and TSEC/KG-84C, also the KIV-7.

1.3.5   Voice encryption

True voice encryption (as opposed to less secure scrambler technology) was pioneered during World War II with the 50-ton SIGSALY, used to protect the very highest level communications. It did not become practical for widespread use until reasonable compact speech encoders became possible in the 1970s.

- STU I and STU II - These systems were expensive and cumbersome and were generally limited to the highest levels of command

- STU-III - These telephone sets operated over ordinary telephone lines and featured the use of security tokens and public key cryptography, making them much more user friendly. They were very popular as a result. Used since the 1980s, this device is rapidly being phased out, and will no longer be supported in the near future.

- 1910 Terminal - Made by a multiple of manufacturers, this device is mostly used as a secure modem. Like the STU-III, new technology has largely eclipsed this device, and it is no longer widely used.

- Secure Terminal Equipment (STE) - This system is intended to replace STU-III. It uses wide-bandwidth voice transmitted over ISDN lines. There is also a version which will communicate over a PSTN (Public Switched Telephone Network) line. It can communicate with STU-III phones and can be upgraded for FNBDT compatibility.

- Sectéra Secure Module - A module that connects to the back of a commercial off the shelf cellular phone. It uses AES or SCIP for encryption.

- OMNI - The OMNI terminal, made by L3 Communications, is another replacement for STU-IIIs. This device uses the FNBDT key and is used to securely send voice and data over the PSTN and ISDN communication systems.

- Secure Iridium - The US Government got a real bargain when it rescued the bankrupt Iridium commercial mobile phone venture. NSA helped add encryption to the Iridium phones.

- KY-57 (VINSON) - One of a series of systems for tactical voice encryption

- HAVE QUICK and SINCGARS use NSA-supplied sequence generators to provide secure frequency hopping

- Future Narrowband Digital Terminal (FNBDT) - Now referred to as the "Secure Communications Interoperability Protocol" (SCIP), the FNBDT is a replacement for the wide-band STE, which uses narrow-bandwidth communications channels like cellular telephone circuits, rather than ISDN lines. The FNBDT/SCIP operates on the application layer of the ISO/OSI Reference Model, meaning that it can be used on top of different types of connections, regardless of the establishment method. It negotiates with the unit at the other end, much like a dial-up modem.

- Fishbowl - In 2012, NSA introduced an Enterprise Mobility Architecture intended to provide a secure VoIP capability using commercial grade products and an Android-based mobile phone called Fishbowl that allows classified communications over commercial wireless networks.[2]

The operational complexity of secure voice played a role in the September 11, 2001 attacks on the United States. According to the 911 Commission, an effective U.S. response was hindered by an inability to set up a secure phone link between the National Military Command Center and the Federal Aviation Administration personnel who were dealing with the hijackings. *See* Communication during the September 11, 2001 attacks.

1.3.6 Internet

NSA has approved a variety of devices for securing Internet Protocol communications. These have been used to secure the Secret Internet Protocol Router Network (SIPRNet), among other uses.

The first commercial network layer encryption device was the Motorola Network Encryption System (NES). The system used the SP3 and KMP protocols defined by the NSA Secure Data Network System (SDNS) and were the direct precursors to IPsec. The NES was built in a three part architecture that used a small cryptographic security kernel to separate the trusted and untrusted network protocol stacks.[3]

The SDNS program defined a Message Security Protocol (MSP) that was built on the use X.509 defined certificates. The first NSA hardware built for this application was the BBN Safekeeper.[4] The Message Security Protocol was a precursor to the IETF Privacy Enhance Mail (PEM) protocol. The BBN Safekeeper provided a high degree of tamper resistance and was one of the first devices used by commercial PKI companies.

1.3.7 Field authentication

NSA still supports simple paper encryption and authentication systems for field use such as DRYAD.

1.3.8 Public systems

NSA has participated in the development of several encryption systems for public use. These include:

- Suite B - a set of public key algorithm standards based on elliptic curve cryptography.

- Advanced Encryption Standard (AES) - an encryption algorithm, selected by NIST after a public competition. In 2003, NSA certified AES for Type 1 use in some NSA-approved systems.

- Secure Hash Algorithm - a widely used family of hash algorithms developed by NSA based on earlier designs by Ron Rivest.

- Digital Signature Algorithm

- Data Encryption Standard (DES)[5]

- Skipjack - the cipher developed for Clipper and finally published in 1998.

- Clipper chip - a controversial failure that convinced NSA that it was advisable to stay out of the public arena.

- Security-Enhanced Linux - not strictly an encryption system, but a recognition that in the 21st century, operating system improvements are more vital to information security than better ciphers.

- The Speck and Simon light-weight Block ciphers, published in 2013.

1.4   References

[1] Melville Klein, "Securing Record Communications: The TSEC/KW-26", 2003, NSA brochure, p. 4, (PDF)

[2] http://www.nsa.gov/ia/_files/Mobility_Capability_Pkg_(Version_1.1U).pdf

[3] http://www.google.com/patents/EP0435094B1

[4] http://books.google.com/books?id=BJVwSRGkDZMC&pg=PA566&lpg=PA566&dq=bbn+safekeeper&source=bl&ots=T6aW1pVfTC sig=4zGegWVGNys0SF10CYyULIp9wc0&hl=en&sa=X&ei=o8sCU-aUGcnloAT-2YKoCQ&ved=0CEEQ6AEwBQ#v=onepage& q=bbn%20safekeeper&f=false

[5] Thomas R. Johnson (2009-12-18). "American Cryptology during the Cold War, 1945-1989.Book III: Retrenchment and Reform, 1972-1980, page 232". NSA, DOCID 3417193 (file released on 2009-12-18, hosted at cryptome.org). Retrieved 2010-01-03.

1.5   Sources

- NSA official site

- Jerry Proc Crypto machine page

- Brooke Clarke Crypto machines site

- Telecommunications Security (TSEC) Nomenclature System

Hand held microprocessor-controlled radios like this AN/PRC-148 have multiple encryption modes.

KY-68 tactical secure telephone.

Chapter 2

AN/CYZ-10

AN/CYZ-10

The **AN/CYZ-10 Data Transfer Device**, often called a **Filler**, **Crazy 10**, **ANCD** or **DTD**, is a United States National Security Agency-developed, portable, hand-held fill device, for securely receiving, storing, and transferring data between compatible cryptographic and communications equipment. It is capable of storing 1,000 keys, maintains an automatic internal audit trail of all security-relevant events that can be uploaded to the LMD/KP, encrypts key for storage, and is programmable. The DTD is capable of keying multiple information systems security (INFOSEC) devices and is compatible with such COMSEC equipment as Single Channel Ground and Airborne Radio System (SINCGARS) radios, KY-57 VINSON, KG-84, and others that are keyed by common fill devices (CFDs). The AN/CYZ-10 supports both the DS-101 and DS-102 interfaces.

The DTD weighs about 4 lb (1.8 kg) and is designed to be fully compatible with future INFOSEC equipment meeting DS-101 signaling and benign fill standards. It will eventually replace the legacy family of CFDs, including the KYK-13, KYX-15 electronic storage devices, and the KOI-18 paper tape reader. Note that only the DTD and the KOI-18 support newer, 128-bit keys.

As of mid-2005, refurbished units cost $4000 each.

The DTD was replaced by the AN/PYQ-10 Simple Key Loader (SKL) which was built and designed by Ralph Osterhout and the Secure DTD2000 System (or SDS), a similarly sized unit that employs the Windows CE operating system. The SDS is currently (2006) beginning production.[1]

2.1   References

[1] http://www.sypriselectronics.com/electronics/content.asp?page_id=34

2.2   External links

-
-
-

Chapter 3

AN/CYZ-9

The **AN/CYZ-9** Random Data Generator is a hardware random number generator fielded by the US National Security Agency in the 1990s. It was used in initial phases of the US military's Electronic Key Management System (EKMS) Tier 2. These systems employ a commercial or militarized personal computer running MS-DOS to generate cryptographic keys and signal operating instructions (SOI/CEOI), with the CYZ-9 producing the needed random bits. The CYZ-9 connects to the PC through an RS-232 port and is powered by five D cell (BA-30) batteries. In later phases of EKMS, the random data functionality is included in an NSA key processor (KP).[1]

3.1 References

[1] http://www.globalsecurity.org/military/library/policy/army/fm/11-1/Ch1.htm US Army Field Manual FM-11-1, 1996, Chapter 1, Section C

Chapter 4

AN/PYQ-10

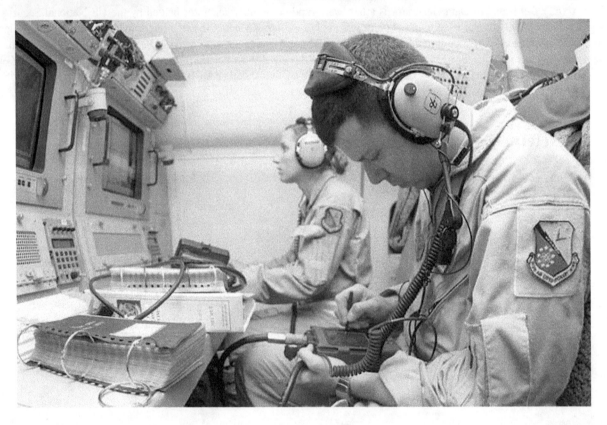

An E-8 crew member entering data using an AN/PYQ-10 before a flight

The **AN/PYQ-10** Simple Key Loader (SKL) is a ruggedized, portable, hand-held fill device, for securely receiving, storing, and transferring data between compatible cryptographic and communications equipment. The SKL was designed and built by Ralph Osterhout and then sold to Sierra Nevada Corporation, with software developed by Science Applications International Corporation (SAIC) under the auspices of the United States Army. It is intended to supplement and eventually replace the AN/CYZ-10 Data Transfer Device (DTD). The PYQ-10 provides all the functions currently resident in the CYZ-10 and incorporates new features that provide streamlined management of COMSEC key, Electronic Protection (EP) data, and Signal Operating Instructions (SOI). Cryptographic functions are performed by an embedded KOV-21 card developed by the National Security Agency (NSA). The AN/PYQ-10 supports both the DS-101 and DS-102 interfaces, as well as the KSD-64 Crypto Ignition Key.[1] The SKL is backward-compatible with existing End Cryptographic Units (ECU) and forward-compatible with future security equipment and systems, including NSA's Key Management

Infrastructure.

Between 2005 and 2007, the U.S. Army budget included funds for over 24,000 SKL units. The estimated price for FY07 was $1708 each. When released in May of 2005, the price was $1695 each. This price includes the unit and the internal encryptor card.[2]

4.1 References

[1] http://www.tobyhanna.army.mil/about/news/cryptographic%20keys.html

[2] "Committee Staff Procurement Backup Book Fiscal Year (FY) 2007 Budget Estimates" (PDF). Dept of the Army. Feb 2006. Retrieved 11 August 2012.

- Serria Nevada SKL spec sheet
- 2005 US Army Weapons System Handbook

Chapter 5

ANDVT

The **Advanced Narrowband Digital Voice Terminal** (ANDVT) is a secure voice terminal for low bandwidth secure voice communications throughout the U.S. Department of Defense. [1] Devices in the ANDVT family include the AN/USC-43 Tactical Terminal (TACTERM), the KY-99A Miniaturized Terminal (MINTERM), and the KY-100 Airborne Terminal (AIRTERM). ANDVT uses LPC-10 voice compression.

The functions of the MINTERM are similar to those of the TACTERM; its updated design includes an improved modular architecture, and it has been reduced in size. The MINTERM is lightweight, low-power, single channel, half-duplex, narrowband/wideband/wireline terminal providing secure voice and data communications with full key distribution and remote rekey capabilities. The MINTERM is certified to secure traffic up to TOP SECRET.

The MINTERM improvements include the following:

- Concurrent voice and data modes enable the users to connect both data equipment and voice handsets.

- VINSON (KY-57/58) mode of operation allows interoperability between the MINTERM and the VINSON wideband COMSEC equipment.

- improved SATCOM performance

- The latest DOD LPC-10 algorithm (V58) which has been enhanced to provide high-quality secure narrowband voice for military handsets and to maintain that quality and intelligibility in noisy acoustical environments.

The AIRTERM is a lightweight, self-contained secure voice and data terminal that provides secure half-duplex voice, digital data, analog data, and remote-keying capabilities for transmission over radio circuits or wireline media. It is a wideband/narrowband terminal that interoperates with the TACTERM, MINTERM, VINSON, and Single Channel Ground and Airborne Radio System (SINCGARS). AIRTERM accepts classified analog voice information and uses LPC-10 at 2.4 kbit/s in narrowband voice modes and continuously variable slope delta (CVSD) modulation at 12 kbit/s and 16 kbit/s in wideband voice modes. The AIRTERM provides the same connectors, with similar functional pinouts, as the VINSON for the wideband operational modes.

5.1 See also

- NSA encryption systems
- FNBDT

5.2 References

[1] "NRL and the Advanced Narrowband Secure Voice Terminal (ANDVT)" (PDF).

5.3 External links

- ANDVT Picture

Chapter 6

Capstone (cryptography)

This article is about the United States government cryptography project. For other uses, see Capstone (disambiguation).

Capstone is the name of a United States government long-term project to develop cryptography standards for public and government use. Capstone was driven by the NIST and the NSA; the project began in 1993. The initiative involved four standard algorithms: a data encryption algorithm called Skipjack, along with the Clipper chip that included the Skipjack algorithm, a digital signature algorithm, DSA, a hash function, SHA-1, and a key exchange protocol. Capstone's first implementation was in the Fortezza PCMCIA card.

The initiative encountered massive resistance from the cryptographic community, and eventually the US government abandoned the effort. The main reasons for this resistance were concerns about Skipjack's design, which was classified, and the use of key escrow in the Clipper chip.

6.1   See also

- Clipper chip
- Skipjack
- Fortezza

6.2   References

- ^ Original press release
- ^ RSA Laboratories FAQ on Cryptography entry
- ^ EFF archives on Capstone

Chapter 7

Clipper chip

Not to be confused with Clipper architecture or Clippy.

The **Clipper chip** was a chipset that was developed and promoted by the United States National Security Agency[1]

MYK-78 "Clipper chip"

(NSA) as an encryption device, with a built-in backdoor, intended to be adopted by telecommunications companies for voice transmission. It was announced in 1993 and by 1996 was entirely defunct.

7.1   Key escrow

The Clipper chip used a data encryption algorithm called Skipjack[1] to transmit information and the Diffie-Hellman key exchange-algorithm to distribute the cryptokeys between the peers. Skipjack was invented by the National Security Agency of the U.S. Government; this algorithm was initially classified SECRET, which prevented it from being subjected to peer review from the encryption research community. The government did state that it used an 80-bit key, that the algorithm was symmetric, and that it was similar to the DES algorithm. The Skipjack algorithm was declassified and published by NSA on June 24, 1998. The initial cost of the chips was said to be $16 (unprogrammed) or $26 (programmed), with its logic designed by Mykotronx, and fabricated by VLSI Technology, Inc (see the VLSI logo on the image this page).

At the heart of the concept was key escrow. In the factory, any new telephone or other device with a Clipper chip would be given a cryptographic key, that would then be provided to the government in escrow. If government agencies "established their authority" to listen to a communication, then the key would be given to those government agencies, who could then decrypt all data transmitted by that particular telephone. The newly formed Electronic Frontier Foundation preferred the term "key surrender" to emphasize what they alleged was really occurring.[2]

7.2   Backlash

Organizations such as the Electronic Privacy Information Center and the Electronic Frontier Foundation challenged the Clipper chip proposal, saying that it would have the effect not only of subjecting citizens to increased and possibly illegal government surveillance, but that the strength of the Clipper chip's encryption could not be evaluated by the public as its design was classified secret, and that therefore individuals and businesses might be hobbled with an insecure communications system. Further, it was pointed out that while American companies could be forced to use the Clipper chip in their encryption products, foreign companies could not, and presumably phones with strong data encryption would be manufactured abroad and spread throughout the world and into the United States, negating the point of the whole exercise, and, of course, materially damaging U.S. manufacturers en route. Then-Senators John Ashcroft and John Kerry were opponents of the Clipper chip proposal, arguing in favor of the individual's right to encrypt messages and export encryption software.[3]

The release and development of several strong cryptographic software packages such as Nautilus, PGP[4] and PGPfone was in response to the government push for the Clipper chip. The thinking was that if strong cryptography was freely available on the internet as an alternative, the government would be unable to stop its use.

7.3   Technical vulnerabilities

In 1994, Matt Blaze published the paper *Protocol Failure in the Escrowed Encryption Standard*.[5] It pointed out that the Clipper's escrow system has a serious vulnerability: the chip transmitted a 128-bit "Law Enforcement Access Field" (LEAF) that contained the information necessary to recover the encryption key. To prevent the software that transmitted the message from tampering with the LEAF, a 16-bit hash was included. The Clipper chip would not decode messages with an invalid hash; however, the 16-bit hash was too short to provide meaningful security. A brute-force attack would quickly produce another LEAF value that would give the same hash but not yield the correct keys after the escrow attempt. This would allow the Clipper chip to be used as an encryption device, while disabling the key escrow capability.[5]:63 In 1995 Yair Frankel and Moti Yung published another attack which shows that the key escrow device tracking and authenticating capability (namely, the LEAF) of one device, can be attached to a messages coming from another device and will nevertheless be received, thus bypassing the escrow in real time. [6] In 1997, a group of leading cryptographers published a paper, "The Risks of Key Recovery, Key Escrow, and Trusted Third-Party Encryption", analyzing the architectural vulnerabilities of implementing key escrow systems in general, including but not limited to the Clipper Chip Skipjack protocol.[7] The technical flaws described in this paper were instrumental in the demise of the Clipper chip as a public policy option. While many leading voices in the computer science community expressed opposition to the Clipper Chip in general and key recovery in general, some supported the concept, including Dorothy E. Denning.[8]

Wired magazine

7.4 Lack of adoption

The Clipper chip was not embraced by consumers or manufacturers and the chip itself was no longer relevant by 1996. The U.S. government continued to press for key escrow by offering incentives to manufacturers, allowing more relaxed export controls if key escrow were part of cryptographic software that was exported. These attempts were largely made moot by the widespread use of strong cryptographic technologies, such as PGP, which were not under the control of the U.S. government. However, strongly encrypted voice channels are still not the predominant mode for current cell phone communications.[9] Secure cell phone devices and smartphone apps exist, but may require specialized hardware, and typically require that both ends of the connection employ the same encryption mechanism. Such apps usually communicate over secure Internet pathways (e.g. ZRTP) instead of through phone voice data networks.

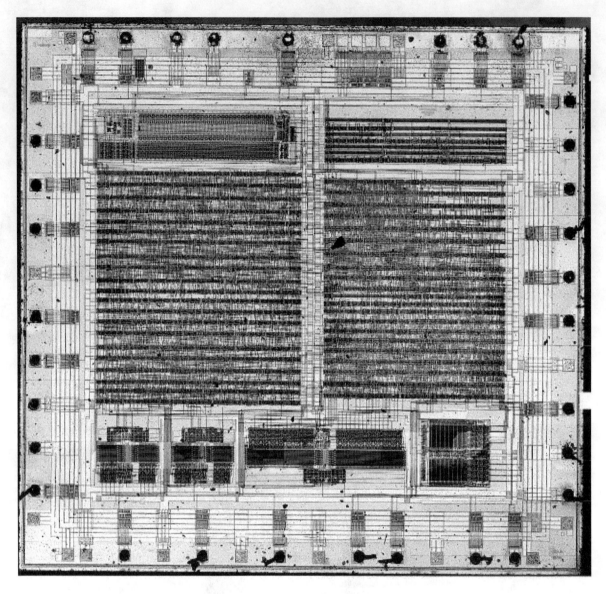

MYK-78

7.5   Later related debates

Following the Snowden disclosures from 2013, Apple and Google announced that they would lock down data stored on their smartphones with encryption, in a way so that Apple and Google could not break the encryption even if ordered to do so with a warrant.[10] This prompted a strong reaction from the authorities, with one of the more iconic responses being the chief of detectives for Chicago's police department stating that "Apple will become the phone of choice for the pedophile".[11] Washington Post posted an editorial insisting that "smartphone users must accept that they cannot be above the law if there is a valid search warrant", and after agreeing that backdoors would be undesirable, suggested implementing a "golden key" backdoor which would unlock the data with a warrant.[12][13] The members of the "The Risks of Key Recovery, Key Escrow, and Trusted Third-Party Encryption" 1997 paper, as well as other researchers at MIT, wrote a follow-up article in response to the revival of this debate, arguing that mandated government access to private conversations would be an even worse problem now than twenty years ago.[14]

7.6   See also

- Bullrun (decryption program)

- Cryptoprocessor

- *Crypto: How the Code Rebels Beat the Government—Saving Privacy in the Digital Age* by Steven Levy

- Trusted Platform Module

7.7   References

[1] "Clipper Chip - Definition of Clipper Chip". computer.yourdictionary.com. Retrieved 2014-01-11.

[2] "Clipper Chip". cryptomuseum.com. Retrieved 2014-01-11.

[3] Summary of Encryption Bills in the 106th Congress

[4] Philip Zimmermann - Why I Wrote PGP (Part of the Original 1991 PGP User's Guide (updated in 1999))

[5] Blaze, Matt (August 20, 1994). "Protocol Failure in the Escrowed Encryption Standard" (PDF). *Proceedings of the 2nd ACM Conference on Computer and Communications Security*: 59–67.

[6] Y. Frankel and M. Yung. Escrow Encryption Systems Visited: Attacks, Analysis and Designs. Crypto 95 Proceedings, August 1995

[7] The Risks of Key Recovery, Key Escrow, and Trusted Third-Party Encryption

[8] Denning, Dorothy E. (July 1995). "The Case for Clipper (Clipper Chip offers escrowed encryption)". *MIT Technology Review*.

[9] Timberg, Craig; Soltani, Ashkan (December 13, 2013), "By cracking cellphone code, NSA has ability to decode private conversations", *The Washington Post*, retrieved August 18, 2015, More than 80 percent of cellphones worldwide use weak or no encryption for at least some of their calls.

[10] http://blog.cryptographyengineering.com/2014/10/why-cant-apple-decrypt-your-iphone.html

[11] http://www.washingtonpost.com/business/technology/2014/09/25/68c4e08e-4344-11e4-9a15-137aa0153527_story.html

[12] http://www.washingtonpost.com/opinions/compromise-needed-on-smartphone-encryption/2014/10/03/96680bf8-4a77-11e4-891d-713f052086i story.html

[13] https://www.techdirt.com/articles/20141006/01082128740/washington-posts-braindead-editorial-phone-encryption-no-backdoors-how-about-m shtml

[14] Abelson, Harold; et al. (July 6, 2015). "Keys Under Doormats: Mandating insecurity by requiring government access to all data and communications". MIT Computer Science and Artificial Intelligence Laboratory.

7.8   External links

- Clipper Chip Q&A

- Clipper Chip White House Statement

- The Evolution of US Government Restrictions on Using and Exporting Encryption Technologies (U), Micheal Schwartzbeck, *Encryption Technologies,* circa 1997, formerly Top Secret, approved for release by NSA with redactions September 10, 2014, C06122418

- Oral history interview with Martin Hellman Oral history interview 2004, Palo Alto, California. Charles Babbage Institute, University of Minnesota, Minneapolis. Hellman describes his invention of public key cryptography with collaborators Whitfield Diffie and Ralph Merkle at Stanford University in the mid-1970s. He also relates his subsequent work in cryptography with Steve Pohlig (the Pohlig-Hellman system) and others. Hellman addresses key escrow (the so-called Clipper chip). He also touches on the commercialization of cryptography with RSA Data Security and VeriSign.

Chapter 8

CONDOR secure cell phone

Qualcomm built several prototype secure CDMA phones for NSA under a contract project called "Condor". The NSA insisted on hardware encryption, which Qualcomm originally implemented using Fortezza PC cards, but later it became apparent that what the NSA really wanted was developed as the STU-III.

8.1 See also

- Secure Communications Interoperability Protocol

- Sectéra Secure Module for Motorola GSM cell phones

Chapter 9

Controlled Cryptographic Item

A **Controlled Cryptographic Item** (CCI) is a U.S. National Security Agency term for secure telecommunications or information handling equipment, associated cryptographic component or other hardware item which performs a critical communications security (COMSEC) function. Items so designated may be unclassified but are subject to special accounting controls and required markings.

Part of the physical security protection given to COMSEC equipment and material is afforded by its special handling and accounting. CCI equipment must be controlled in a manner that affords protection at least equal to that normally provided other high value equipment, such as money, computers, and Privacy Act-controlled. There are two separate channels used for the handling of such equipment and materials: "the COMSEC channel" and "the administrative channel." The COMSEC channel, called the COMSEC Material Control System, is used to distribute accountable COMSEC items such as classified and CCI equipment, keying material, and maintenance manuals. Some military departments have been authorized to distribute CCI equipment through their standard logistics system.

The COMSEC channel is composed of a series of COMSEC accounts, each of which has an appointed COMSEC Custodian who is personally responsible and accountable for all COMSEC materials charged to his/her account. The COMSEC Custodian assumes accountability for the equipment or material upon receipt, then controls its dissemination to authorized individuals on job requirements and a need-to-know basis. The administrative channel is used to distribute COMSEC information other than that which is accountable in the COMSEC Material Control System.

Persons with access to COMSEC materials are asked, among other restrictions, to avoid unapproved travel to any countries which are adversaries of the United States, or their establishments or facilities within the U.S.[1]

9.1 References

[1] U.S. DOD Controlled Cryptographic Item Briefing Form DD2625

Chapter 10

DRYAD

This article is about the enciphering system. For other uses, see Dryad (disambiguation).

The **DRYAD Numeral Cipher/Authentication System (KTC 1400 D)** is a simple, paper cryptographic system employed by the U.S. military for authentication and for encryption of short, numerical messages. Each unit with a radio is given a set of matching DRYAD code sheets. A single sheet is valid for a limited time (e.g. 6 hours), called a *cryptoperiod*.

A DRYAD cipher sheet contains 25 lines or rows of scrambled letters. Each line is labeled by the letters A to Y in a column on the left of the page. Each row contains a random permutation of the letters A through Y. The letters in each row are grouped into 10 columns labeled 0 through 9. The columns under 0, 1, 2 and 5 have more letters than the other digits, which have just two each.

While crude, the DRYAD Numeral Cipher/Authentication System has the advantage of being fast, relatively easy and requires no extra equipment (such as a pencil). The presence of more cipher-text columns under the digits 0, 1, 2 and 5, is apparently intended to make ciphertext frequency analysis more difficult. But much of the security comes from keeping the cryptoperiod short.

DRYAD can be used in two modes, authentication or encryption.

10.1 Authentication

For authentication, a challenging station selects a letter at random from the left most column followed by a second (randomly selected) letter in the row of the first chosen letter. The station being challenged would then authenticate by picking the letter directly below the row and position of the second letter selected.[1][2]

For example, using the example cipher sheet to the right and the NATO phonetic alphabet, Jason could challenge Peggy by transmitting "authenticate Alpha Bravo". Peggy's correct response would then be "authenticate Yankee".

Another form used involves selecting the third letter to the right of the second letter chosen by the challenging station (Jason's "Bravo" letter). Both the directional offset (up, down, left or right) and numeral offset can be different values then the examples given here; but must be agreed upon and understood by both parties before authentication.

One problem presented is that an enemy impersonator has a one in 25 chance of guessing the correct response (one in 24 if a letter is selected from the same row). A solution to this is for Jason to require Peggy to authenticate twice; lowering the impersonator's odds of guessing the correct response to one in 625. The downside to this method is reduced longevity of the current DRYAD page, since the page is getting twice as much use as a single-authentication scheme.

10.2   Encryption

The second mode is used to encrypt short numeric information (such as map coordinates or a new radio frequency). The coder selects two letters at random. The first selects a row in the current active page. The second letter is used as in the authentication mode, except the adjacent letter to the right is the one selected; and is called the "SET LETTER."

Numbers are enciphered one digit at a time. A ciphertext letter is chosen from the selected row in the column under the plain text digit. If the digit occurs more than once in the number, the coder is instructed to choose a different letter in the same column. All the digits in a single plaintext number are encoded from the same row. (There is also a provision for encoding letters associated with map grid coordinates.)

10.3   See also

- BATCO — similar paper based tactical cipher used by the British forces

- M-94 — tactical cipher used in WWII

- Dryad — original meaning in mythology

- Polyalphabetic cipher

- Substitution cipher

10.4   References

[1] Army Field Manual 24-19, Chapter 5

[2] U.S. Army Field Manual FM 24-12, Chapter 7, Communications Security Operations

- Further explanation of the DRYAD Numeral Cipher/Authentication System

- U.S. Army Field Manual FM 24-35

FOR OFFICIAL USE ONLY
(PROTECTIVE MARKING)

KTV 14000

	ABC 0	DEF 1	GHJ 2	KI 3	MN 4	PQR 5	ST 6	UV 7	WX 8	YZ 9
A	ERSQ	WOJ	NKI	PB	YD	MTA	GU	HV	XF	LC
B	GJNH	ULF	EKA	OY	VB	STC	DI	QP	WR	XM
C	DAFH	CUB	TKM	OR	NE	GXQ	VY	IL	SP	JW
D	RMXF	IVO	TQY	WS	JP	LBD	CK	GE	HU	NA
E	IATL	DVO	SWX	MH	KQ	EYF	RN	BC	PU	JG
F	RCMX	AGO	TIE	NF	PH	YDB	QV	LX	UJ	SW

	ABC 0	DEF 1	GHJ 2	KI 3	MN 4	PQR 5	ST 6	UV 7	WX 8	YZ 9
G	TYKN	AHE	VUQ	IM	FD	RCW	BO	XP	JS	LG
H	AHOG	CKS	PNU	BR	DT	MYX	EQ	FL	VW	JI
I	OWGJ	SXC	DAP	RE	LY	QUF	MV	NB	TH	IK
J	YNAT	GBD	LOF	EJ	RS	MIK	WH	PQ	XU	VC
K	LYQE	UVN	JIC	HM	AG	KTP	DW	OX	SR	FB
L	GQCN	HUI	SMR	JB	FO	XWY	VT	EA	KL	PD

	ABC 0	DEF 1	GHJ 2	KI 3	MN 4	PQR 5	ST 6	UV 7	WX 8	YZ 9
M	CLUR	TJN	VAF	EX	DW	QKH	MP	GB	YI	OS
N	RPJU	QHX	CTN	OW	MA	KBV	EL	IG	SD	FY
O	QTOY	XMK	AWN	RJ	EF	PLS	DV	HB	CI	UG
P	PWMR	IEJ	ADK	GH	TS	QYC	ON	BU	LF	VX
Q	JRDA	QFN	BOI	SM	WH	KCX	GP	VL	YT	EU
R	MPBR	WXC	VJD	UN	KG	HQF	SE	LI	AY	TO

	ABC 0	DEF 1	GHJ 2	KI 3	MN 4	PQR 5	ST 6	UV 7	WX 8	YZ 9
S	YPFV	DLU	QKT	HR	EO	ASI	CG	XN	MJ	WB
T	NCRT	DOG	UYX	BE	WJ	FSH	QP	LI	VM	AK
U	EBJR	IHV	YGL	AQ	NC	WPS	UX	KD	FO	TM
V	JOTC	VAB	DIR	FS	LW	QHU	EP	XY	KN	GM
W	AOCN	WJL	KDB	PI	RV	FGQ	UH	SM	XT	YE
X	SVHC	EML	YOA	GU	DK	FXI	JN	WT	PB	RQ
Y	EBOH	STL	FIM	GW	PY	JVA	UR	DN	KX	QC

FOR OFFICIAL USE ONLY

A sample DRYAD cipher sheet

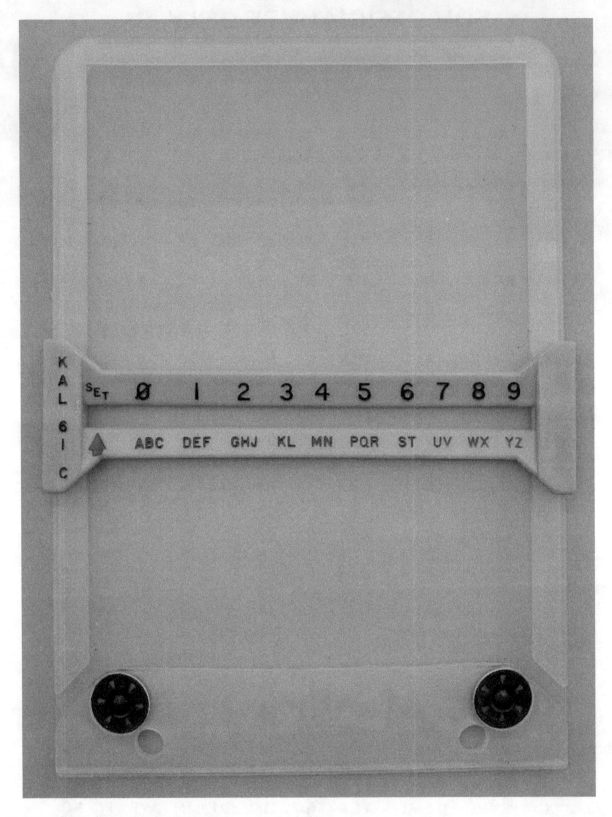

Holder for coding sheets with slide to facilitate use

Chapter 11

FASCINATOR

FASCINATOR is a series of Type 1 encryption modules designed in the late-1980s to be installed in Motorola digital-capable voice radios. These radios were originally built to accept a DES-based encryption module that was not approved by NSA for classified communications. The FASCINATOR modules replaced the DES units and can be used for classified conversations at all levels when used with appropriately classified keys. FASCINATOR operates at 12 kbit/s for encryption and decryption. It is not compatible with DES-based voice systems.

NSA originally supplied keys for FASCINATOR on paper tape for loading using KOI-18 or KYK-13 fill devices and a special adaptor box and cable. The standard cryptoperiod was 7 days, i.e. keys had to be changed weekly.

FASCINATOR was adopted by the U.S government as Federal Standard 1023, which establishes interoperability requirements regarding the analog to digital conversion, encryption (with related synchronization), and modulation of encrypted voice associated with frequency modulation (FM) radio systems employing 25 kHz channels and operating above 30 MHz. Voice is digitized using 12 kbit/s continuously variable slope delta modulation (CVSD) and then encrypted using a National Security Agency (NSA) Commercial COMSEC Endorsement Program (CCEP) Type 1 encryption algorithm based on the KY-57/58.

11.1   Sources

- Operational Security Policy for Communications Equipment with FASCINATOR, US Marine Corps order 2231.2, 1989

- FED-STD 1023 Telecommunications: Interoperability Requirements For Encrypted, Digitized Voice Utilized With 25 kHz Channel FM Radios Operating Above 30 MHz

Chapter 12

Fill device

KY-57 voice encryptor. Note fill port in center.

A **fill device** is an electronic module used to load cryptographic keys into electronic encryption machines. Fill devices are usually hand held and battery operated.

Older mechanical encryption systems, such as rotor machines, were keyed by setting the positions of wheels and plugs from a printed keying list. Electronic systems required some way to load the necessary cryptovariable data. In the 1950s and 1960s, systems such as the U.S. National Security Agency KW-26 and the Soviet Union's Fialka used punched cards for this purpose. Later NSA encryption systems incorporated a serial port fill connector and developed several **common fill devices** (CFDs) that could be used with multiple systems. A CFD was plugged in when new keys were to be loaded. Newer NSA systems allow "over the air rekeying" (OTAR), but a master key often must still be loaded using a fill device.

A KYK-13 fill device.

NSA uses two serial protocols for key fill, **DS-101** and **DS-102**. Both employ the same U-229 6-pin connector type used for U.S. military audio handsets, with the DS-101 being the newer of the two serial fill protocols. The DS-101 protocol can also be used to load cryptographic algorithms and software updates for crypto modules.

Besides encryption devices, systems that can require key fill include IFF, GPS and frequency hopping radios such as Have Quick and SINCGARS.

Common fill devices employed by NSA include:

- KYK-13 Electronic Transfer Device
- KYX-15 Net Control Device[1]
- MX-10579 ECCM Fill Device (SINCGARS)[2]
- KOI-18 paper tape reader. The operator pulls 8-level tape through this unit by hand.
- AN/CYZ-10 Data Transfer Device - a small PDA-like unit that can store up to 1000 keys.
- Secure DTD2000 System (SDS) - Named KIK-20, this was the next generation common fill device replacement for the DTD when it started production in 2006. It employs the Windows CE operating system.[3]
- AN/PYQ-10 Simple Key Loader (SKL) - a simpler replacement for the DTD.
- KSD-64 Crypto ignition key (CIK)
- KIK-30, a more recent fill device, is trademarked as the "Really Simple Key Loader" (RASKL) with "single button key-squirt." It supports a wide variety of devices and keys.[4]

The older KYK-13,[5] KYX-15 and MX-10579 are limited to certain key types.

12.1   See also

- List of cryptographic key types

12.2   References

[1] http://www.jproc.ca/crypto/kyx15.html

[2] http://www.prc68.com/I/MX18290.shtml

[3] http://www.securecomm.com/sds2000.html

[4] http://www.sypris.com/filemanager/library/syp-19787-raskl-brochure.pdf

[5] http://www.cryptomuseum.com/crypto/usa/kyk13/index.htm

12.3   External links

- Fill devices
- KYX-15 pictures

Chapter 13

Fishbowl (secure phone)

Fishbowl is a mobile phone architecture developed by the U.S. National Security Agency (NSA) to provide a secure Voice over IP (VoIP) capability using commercial grade products that can be approved to communicate classified information. It is the first phase of NSA's Enterprise Mobility Architecture. According to a presentation at the 2012 RSA Conference by Margaret Salter, a Technical Director in the Information Assurance Directorate, "The plan was to buy commercial components, layer them together and get a secure solution. It uses solely commercial infrastructure to protect classified data." Government employees were reportedly testing 100 of the phones as of the announcement.[1]

The initial version was implemented using Google's Android operating system, modified to ensure central control of the phone's configuration at all times. To minimize the chance of compromise, the phones use two layers of encryption protocols, IPsec and Secure Real-time Transport Protocol (SRTP), and employ NSA's Suite B encryption and authentication algorithms.

The phones are locked down in many ways. While they use commercial wireless channels, all communications must be sent through an enterprise-managed server. No direct voice calls are allowed, except for 9-1-1 emergency calls. Only NSA approved applications from the NSA enterprise app store can be installed. NSA has published a 100-page overview specification for the Mobility Capability Package.[2] In tandem with the Capability Package there are a series of Protection Profiles. [3] These Protection Profiles list out the requirements a commercial product must meet to be used in the mobile phone architecture.

13.1 References

[1] http://www.scmagazine.com.au/News/292189,nsa-builds-android-phone-for-top-secret-calls.aspx NSA builds Android phone for top secret calls

[2] http://www.nsa.gov/ia/_files/Mobility_Capability_Pkg_Vers_2_1.pdf

[3] https://www.niap-ccevs.org/pp/index.cfm?&CFID=18170027&CFTOKEN=640af50d25b9baa2-3B6BCE4B-C0B3-B411-7F8F85AB279753Dt

Chapter 14

Fortezza

This article is about Fortezza the security system. For town in Italy, see Franzensfeste.

Fortezza is an information security system[1] that uses the **Fortezza Crypto Card**, a PC Card-based security token.[2]

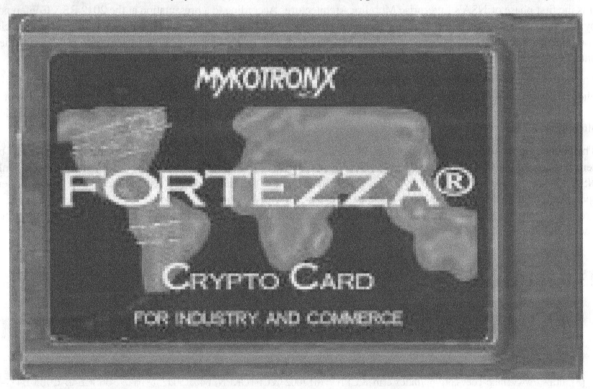

A Fortezza card made by Mykotronx Corp.

It was developed for the U.S. government's Clipper chip project and has been used by the U.S. Government in various applications.

Each individual who is authorized to see protected information is issued a *Fortezza card* that stores private keys and other data needed to gain access. It contains an NSA approved security microprocessor called *Capstone* (MYK-80) that implements the Skipjack encryption algorithm.

The original Fortezza card (KOV-8) is a Type 2 product which means it cannot be used for classified information. The most widely used Type 1 encryption card is the KOV-12 Fortezza card which is used extensively for the Defense Message System (DMS). The KOV-12 is cleared up to TOP SECRET/SCI. A later version, called KOV-14 or **Fortezza Plus**, uses a Krypton microprocessor that implements stronger, Type 1 encryption and may be used for information classified up to TOP SECRET/SCI. It, in turn, is being replaced by the newer KSV-21 PC card with more modern algorithms and additional capabilities. The cards are interchangeable within the many types of equipment that support Fortezza and can be rekeyed and reprogrammed by the owners, making them easy to issue and reuse. This simplifies the process of rekeying equipment for crypto changes: instead of requiring an expensive fill device, a technician is able to put a new Fortezza card in the device's PCMCIA slot.

The Fortezza Plus card and its successors are used with NSA's Secure Terminal Equipment voice and data encryption systems that are replacing the STU-III. It is manufactured by the Mykotronx Corporation and by Spyrus. Each card costs about $240 and they are commonly used with card readers sold by Litronic Corporation.

The Fortezza card has been used in government, military, and banking applications to protect sensitive data.[3]

14.1 References

[1] Shirey, Robert (August 2007). "Definitions". *Internet Security Glossary, Version 2*. IETF. p. 133. RFC 4949. https://tools.ietf.org/html/rfc4949#page-133. Retrieved February 16, 2012.

[2] "FIPS-140-1 Security and FORTEZZA Crypto Cards". *Choosing Security Solutions That Use Public Key Technology*. Microsoft. Retrieved February 16, 2012.

[3] John R. Vacca (May 1995). "NSA provides value-added crypto security - National Security Agency; Group Technology's Fortezza Crypto Card". *Communications News*. Nelson Publishing. Retrieved February 16, 2012.

- "FORTEZZA crypto card". *Jane's Military Communications*. Jane's Information Group. Aug 10, 2009. Retrieved February 16, 2012.

- Workstation Security Products Division (2 January 1997). "Basic Certification Requirements for FORTEZZA™ Applications". National Security Agency. Retrieved February 16, 2012.

- "FORTEZZA". Rainbow Technologies. Retrieved February 16, 2012.

- "Fortezza Crypto Card". Crypto Museum. Retrieved February 16, 2012.

- Kenneth W. Dam and Herbert S. Lin, ed. (1996). "The Capstone/Fortezza Initiative". *Cryptography's role in securing the information society*. National Research Council. Washington, DC: National Academy Press. pp. 176–177. ISBN 978-0-309-05475-1. Retrieved 16 February 2012.

- Peter Gutmann (2004). "The Capstone/Fortezza Generator". *Cryptographic security architecture: design and verification*. New York: Springer. pp. 236–237. ISBN 978-0-387-95387-8. Retrieved 16 February 2012.

14.2 External links

- SafeNet web site (Mykotronx is a division of SafeNet)
- Spyrus web site
- Litronic web site

Chapter 15

General Dynamics C4 Systems

General Dynamics C4 Systems is a business unit of American defense and aerospace company General Dynamics. General Dynamics C4 Systems is a leading integrator of secure communication and information systems and technology. General Dynamics C4 Systems has core manufacturing in secure communications networks; radios and satellite technology for the military, public safety, and scientific communities.

15.1 History

General Dynamics C4 Systems was originally owned by GTE and operated as GTE Government Systems. General Dynamics acquired GTE Government Systems in 1999.[1]

- NOTE: This history needs investigation & update to show General Dynamics' purchase of the Motorola Integrated Information Systems Group (IISG) in 2001 as the General Dynamics Decision Systems business unit and the later merger with GDC4S.

15.2 Products

- TACLANE - Network encryption device developed with the NSA

- Sectera - Portable secure voice and data device developed for the NSA

- CoMotion

- ModIOS - Defense Information System Simulation Management tool for Windows and UNIX®. As one of the most comprehensive exercise management software packages commercially available, ModIOS provides the network interface to simulation, exercise control functions, 2D and 3D views, recording and playback of simulated exercises, voice communications and after action review debriefs/reports.

- S2Focus - Commercial-Off-The-Shelf (COTS) software tool suite that provides the critical infrastructure necessary to conduct distributed simulations and training. Key capabilities include data recording, data analysis, data filtering and control, data visualization, mission planning, learning content management, and user progress tracking.

15.3 References

[1] http://www.purchasing.com/article/226738-General_Dynamics_decentralizes_e_sourcing.php

15.4 External links

- General Dynamics C4 Systems Website

Chapter 16

High Assurance Internet Protocol Encryptor

A **High Assurance Internet Protocol Encryptor** (**HAIPE**) is a Type 1 encryption device that complies with the National Security Agency's HAIPE IS (formerly the HAIPIS, the High Assurance Internet Protocol Interoperability Specification). The cryptography used is Suite A and Suite B, also specified by the NSA as part of the Cryptographic Modernization Program. HAIPE IS is based on IPsec with additional restrictions and enhancements. One of these enhancements includes the ability to encrypt multicast data using a "preplaced key" (see definition in List of cryptographic key types). This requires loading the same key on all HAIPE devices that will participate in the multicast session in advance of data transmission. A HAIPE is typically a secure gateway that allows two enclaves to exchange data over an untrusted or lower-classification network.

Examples of HAIPE devices include:

- L-3 Communications' HAIPE [1]
  - KG-245X 10Gbit/s (HAIPE IS v3.0.2),
  - KG-245A fully tactical 1 Gbit/s (HAIPE IS v3.1.2 and Foreign Interoperable)
  - KG-240A fully ruggedized 100 Mbit/s (HAIPE IS v3.1.2 and Foreign Interoperable)
  - KOV-26 TALON [2]
- ViaSat's AltaSec Products[3]
  - KG-250,[4] and
  - KG-255 [1 Gbit/s][5]
- General Dynamics' TACLANE KG-175[6]
- Airbus Defence & Space ECTOCRYP Transparent Cryptography [7][8]

Three of these devices are compliant to the HAIPE IS v3.0.2 specification while the remaining devices use the HAIPE IS version 1.3.5, which has a couple of notable limitations: no support for routing protocols or open network management.

A HAIPE is an IP encryption device, looking up the destination IP address of a packet in its internal Security Association Database (SAD) and picking the encrypted tunnel based on the appropriate entry. For new communications, HAIPEs use the internal Security Policy Database (SPD) to set up new tunnels with the appropriate algorithms and settings. By not supporting routing protocols the HAIPEs must be preprogrammed with static routes and cannot adjust to changing network topology. While manufacturers support centralized management of their devices through proprietary software,[9][10] the current devices offer no management functionality through open protocols or standards.

TELEGRID Technologies[11] produces a non proprietary Encryptor Management System for multiple INE, HAIPE and Mobile IP encryptors including the KIV-7M, GD KG-175D, ViaSat KG-250 and Harris SecNet54. The Encryptor Management System is known as the Secure Multi-web Remoting Tool (SMRT).[12] The SMRT provides an encryptor management interface as well as a common crypto MIB for remote management via SNMP. It also provides secure remote access to the management interfaces of the underlying encryptors.

Both the HAIPE IS v3 management and HAIPE device implementations are required to be compliant to the HAIPE IS version 3.0 common MIBs. Assurance of cross vendor interoperability may require additional effort. An example of a management application that supports HAIPE IS v3 is the L-3 Common HAIPE Manager.

A couple of new HAIPE devices will combine the functionality of a router and encryptor when HAIPE IS version 3.0 is approved. General Dynamics has completed its TACLANE version (KG-175R), which house both a red and a black Cisco router, and both ViaSat and L-3 Communications are coming out with a line of network encryptors at version 3.0 and above. Cisco is partnering with Harris Corporation to propose a solution called SWAT1[13]

There is a UK HAIPE variant that implements UKEO algorithms in place of US Suite A. Cassidian has entered the HAIPE market in the UK with its Ectocryp range. Ectocryp Blue is HAIPE version 3.0 compliant and provides a number of the HAIPE extensions as well as support for network quality of service (QoS). Harris has also entered the UK HAIPE market with the BID/2370 End Cryptographic Unit (ECU).[14]

In addition to site encryptors HAIPE is also being inserted into client devices that provide both wired and wireless capabilities. Examples of these include L-3 Communication's KOV-26 Talon and Guardian SME-PED, and Harris Corporation's KIV-54 [15] and PRC-117G [16] radio.

16.1   See also

- NSA encryption systems

16.2   References

[1] L-3 Common HAIPE Manager

[2] L-3 Talon

[3] ViaSat Information Assurance web page

[4] ViaSat KG-250

[5] ViaSat KG-255

[6] General Dynamics TACLANE Encryptor (KG-175)

[7] Ectocrypt Blue by Cassidian, an EADS Company

[8] "CASSIDIAN unveils ECTOCRYP YELLOW". September 2013.

[9] ViaSat's VINE website

[10] General Dynamics's GEM website

[11] TELEGRID Technologies

[12] TELEGRID SMRT Multiple HAIPE Remote Manager

[13] Cisco Harris SWAT1 Solution

[14] Harris UK BID/2370 ECU

[15] Harris KIV-54 (SECNET 54)

[16] Harris AN/PRC-117G

16.3   External links

- CNSS Policy #19 governing the use of HAIPE

Chapter 17

KG-84

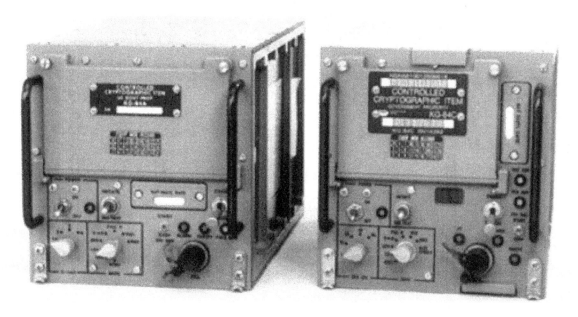

KG-84A and KG-84C. US Navy photo.

The **KG-84A** and **KG-84C** are encryption devices developed by the U.S. National Security Agency (NSA) to ensure secure transmission of digital data. The KG-84C is a Dedicated Loop Encryption Device (DLED), and both devices are General-Purpose Telegraph Encryption Equipment (GPTEE). The KG-84A is primarily used for point-to-point encrypted communications via landline, microwave, and satellite systems. The KG-84C is an outgrowth of the U.S. Navy high frequency (HF) communications program and supports these needs. The KG-84A and KG-84C are devices that operate in simplex, half-duplex, or full-duplex modes. The KG-84C contains all of the KG-84 and KG-84A modes, plus a variable update counter, improved HF performance, synchronous out-of-sync detection, asynchronous cipher text, plain text, bypass, and European TELEX protocol. The KG-84 (A/C) is certified to handle data at all levels of security. The KG-84 (A/C) is a Controlled Cryptographic Item (CCI) and is unclassified when unkeyed. Keyed KG-84 equipment assumes the classification level equal to that of the keying material used.

17.1   Characteristics

17.1.1   KG-84 A/C physical characteristics

- Height 7.8 in (198 mm)

- Width 7.5 in (191 mm)

- Depth 15 in (381 mm)

- Weight 23 lb (10 kg)

17.1.2   Data rate

- KG-84A 256 kbit/s synchronous and 9.6 kbit/s asynchronous

- KG-84C Up to 64 kbit/s synchronous and 9.6 kbit/s asynchronous

17.1.3   Power

- 24 V DC, 15 W

- 115 V AC

- 220 V AC

17.1.4   Operating temperature

Operating temperature: 0 to 55 °C

17.1.5   MTBF

69,000 hours (7.9 years)

17.2   See also

- NSA encryption systems

17.3   External links

- More info on KG-84; see also .

- Information

Chapter 18

KIK-30

The **KIK-30** "Really Simple Key loader" (RASKL) is a fill device made by Sypris Electronics and approved by the US National Security Agency for the distribution of NSA Type 1 cryptographic keys. It can also store and transfer related communications security material, including control data ("load sets") for frequency hopping radios, such as SINCGARS and Have Quick.[1] It can store up to 40 cryptographic keys and has male and female U-229 connectors for the NSA DS-101 and 102 fill protocol, allowing it to be plugged into most other NSA fill devices and EKMS equipment. It is 6.14 inches (159 mm) long, weighs less than one pound (454 g) and is powered by four AAA batteries. The operator interface has an 8 line of 20 characters and 6 buttons, with what Sypris calls "1-button key squirt" and 2-button zeroize (clear memory).[2]

A simpler device than the AN/CYZ-10, the KIK-30 is now planned to replace the venerable KYK-13 fill devices, with up to $200 million budgeted in 2009 to procure the newer units in quantity.[3]

18.1 References

[1] KIK-30 The First Modernized KYK-13 Replacement

[2] https://www.sypriselectronics.com/media/5711/syp-19787-raskl-brochure.pdf

[3] http://defensesystems.com/articles/2009/11/12/dod-cryptographic-key.aspx

Chapter 19

KIV-7

The **KIV-7** is a National Security Agency Type-1, single-channel encryptor originally designed in the mid-1990s by AlliedSignal Corporation to meet the demand for secure data communications from personal computers (PC), workstations, and FAXs. It has data rates up to 512 kbit/s and is interoperable with the KG-84, KG-84A, and KG-84C data encryption devices.

19.1   Versions

Several versions of the KIV-7 have been developed over the years by many different corporations that have either bought the rights to build the KIV-7 or through corporate mergers.

- KIV-7 Speeds up to 512 kbit/s

- KIV-7 HS Speeds up to T-1 (1.54 Mbit/s)

- KIV-7HSB Speeds up to 2.048 Mbit/s

- KIV-7M Speeds up to 50 Mbit/s and supports the High Assurance Internet Protocol Interoperability Specification (HAIPIS)

(The National Security Agency (NSA) has established new High Assurance Internet Protocol Interoperability Specifications (HAIPIS) that requires different vendor's Inline Network Encryption (INE) devices to be interoperable.)

19.2   References

- HAIPE

- Committee on National Security Systems (CNSS Policy No. 19)

- Cryptography

- NSA encryption systems

- SafeNet Mykotronx, manufacturer of a line of KIV-7 devices.

19.3   External links

- CNSS Policy No. 19, National Policy Governing the Use of High Assurance Internet Protocol Encryptor (HAIPE) Products

Chapter 20

KL-43

The **KL-43** is a portable, electronic cipher device used by the United States and the NATO from the early 1980s. The machine, manufactured by TRW, is an adaptation of language translator technology, and includes a keyboard for input and an LCD for output. It also contains a built-in modem, a telephone coupler, and the facility for connecting to a printer. A version of the KL-43 was famously used by Oliver North to communicate with his assistant, Fawn Hall, and others while managing clandestine operations in Nicaragua in support of the "Contra" rebels. The device was paraded in front of cameras during the Iran-Contra congressional hearings.

There are a number of variations of the KL-43, including the following:

- KL-43A - early model.

- KL-43C - a tactical rugged version from the 1980s.

- KL-43D - mid-production and most common version with small keyboard (original cost ca. US$300).

- KL-43E - full-size keyboard model for high volume office operations (original cost below US$1000).

- KL-43F - most recent tactical version for wired and wireless networks made by EPI.

20.1 External links

- LTC David Fiedler, The KL-43: burst communications on a budget, Army Communicator, Winter/Spring 1990, Vol. 15 No. 1.

- Jerry Proc's page on the KL-43

- NATO's KL-43C/F description

A KL-43 on display at the National Cryptologic Museum.

Chapter 21

KL-51

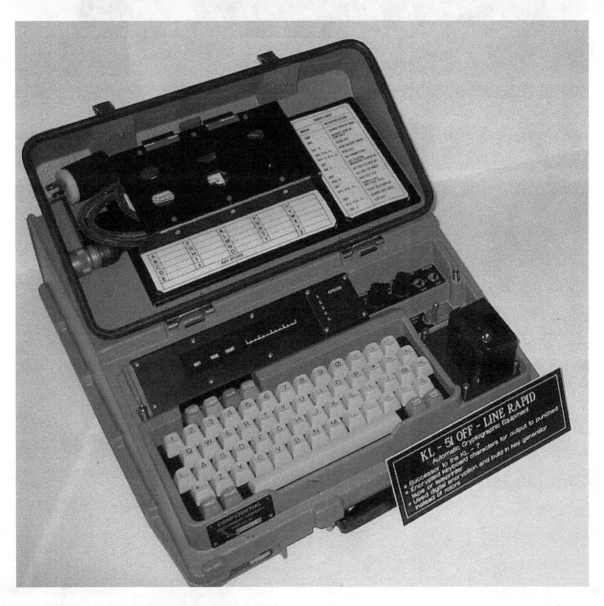

KL-51 on display at the National Cryptologic Museum in 2005.

The **KL-51** is an off-line keyboard encryption system that read and punched paper tape for use with teleprinters. In NATO it was called **RACE** (**Rapid Automatic Cryptographic Equipment**).

It was developed in the 1970s by a Norwegian company, Standard Telefon og Kabelfabrik (STK). It used digital electronics for encryption instead of rotors, and it may have been the first machine to use software based crypto algorithms. KL-51 is a very robust machine made to military specifications.

U.S. National Security Agency bought it in the 1980s to replace the earlier KL-7. As of 2006, the U.S. Navy was developing plans to replace KL-51 units still in use with a unit based on a more modern Universal Crypto Device.[1]

21.1 References

[1] http://www.dtic.mil/descriptivesum/Y2007/Navy/0303140N.pdf

21.2 Sources

- NSA museum caption shown in photo.

- Crypto Machines - KL-51/RACE

- http://www.knobstick.ca/pdf_files/race1.pdf

Chapter 22

KL-7

A KL-7 on display aboard HMS Belfast.

The **TSEC/KL-7**, code named **ADONIS** and **POLLUX**, was an off-line non-reciprocal rotor encryption machine.[1] The KL-7 had eight rotors to encrypt the text, seven of which moved in a complex pattern, controlled by notched rings. The non-moving rotor was in fourth from the left of the stack. The encrypted or decrypted output of the machine was printed on a small paper ribbon. It was the first cipher machine to use the re-entry (re-flexing) principle, discovered by Albert W. Small,[2] which re-introduces the encryption output back into the encryption process to re-encipher it again.

The research for the new cipher machine, designated MX-507, was initiated in 1945 by the Army Security Agency (ASA) as a successor for the SIGABA and the less secure Hagelin M-209. Its development was turned over to the newly formed Armed Forces Security Agency (AFSA) in 1949. The machine was renamed AFSAM-7, which stands for Armed Forces Security Agency Machine No 7. It was the first crypto machine, developed under one centralized cryptologic organisation as a standard machine for all parts of the armed forces, and it was the first cipher machine to use electronics (vacuum tubes).

In 1952, the machine was introduced by AFSA's successor, the U.S. National Security Agency, in the US Army, Navy and Air Force. In the early 1960s, the AFSAM-7 was renamed TSEC/KL-7, following the new standard crypto nomenclature. It was the most widely used crypto machine in the US armed forces until the mid-1960s. The KL-7 was also used by several NATO countries until 1983.

22.1 Description

The KL-7 was designed for off-line operation. It was about the size of a Teletype machine and had a similar three-row keyboard, with shift keys for letters and figures. The KL-7 produced printed output on narrow paper strips that were then glued to message pads. When encrypting, it automatically inserted a space between five-letter code groups. One of the reasons for the five letter groups was messages might be given to a morse code operator. The number of five letter groups was easily verified when transmitted. There was an adaptor available, the **HL-1/X22**, that allowed 5-level Baudot punched paper tape from Teletype equipment to be read for decryption. The standard KL-7 had no ability to punch tapes. A variant of the KL-7, the **KL-47**, could also punch paper tape for direct input to teleprinters.

Both sides of a KL-7 rotor

Each rotor had 36 contacts. To establish a new encryption setting, operators would select a rotor and place it in a plastic outer ring at a certain offset. The ring and the offset to use for each position were specified in a printed key list. This process would be repeated eight times until all rotor positions were filled. Key settings were usually changed every day at midnight, GMT. The basket containing the rotors was removable, and it was common to have a second basket and set of rotors, allowing the rotors to be set up prior to key change. The old basket could then be kept intact for most of the day to decode messages sent the previous day, but received after midnight.

The keyboard itself was a large sliding switch, also called permutor board. A signal, coming from a letter key, went through the rotors, back to the permutor board to continue to the printer. The KL-7 was non-reciprocal. Therefore, depending on the *Encipher* or *Decipher* position of the permutor board, the direction of the signal through the rotors was changed.

The rotor basket had two sets of connectors, two with 26 pins and two with 10 pins, at each end that mated with the main assembly. Both 26 pin connectors were connected to the keyboard to enable the switching of the signal direction through the rotors. Both 10 pin connectors on each side were hard-wired with each other. If a signal that entered on one of the 26 pins left the rotor pack on one of these 10 pins, that signal was redirected back into the rotors on the entry side to perform a new pass through the rotors. This loop-back, the so-called re-entry, created complex scrambling of the signal and could result in multiple passes through the rotor pack, depending on the current state of the rotor wiring.

There was also a switch pile-up under each movable rotor that was operated by cams on its plastic outer ring. Different outer rings had different arrangements of cams. The circuitry of the switches controlled solenoids which in turn enabled the movement of the rotors. The combination of cam rings and the controlling of a rotor by several switches created a most complex and irregular stepping. The exact wiring between switches and solenoids is still classified.

KL-7 on display at USAF Communications Agency museum. Rotors have been removed.

The KL-7 was largely replaced by electronic systems such as the KW-26 ROMULUS and the KW-37 JASON in the 1970s, but KL-7s were kept in service as backups and for special uses. In 1967, when John Anthony Walker (a sailor in the U.S. Navy) walked into the embassy of the Soviet Union in Washington, DC seeking employment as a spy, he carried with him a copy of a key list for the KL-47. KL-7s were compromised at other times as well. A unit captured by North Vietnam is on display at NSA's National Cryptologic Museum. The KL-7 was withdrawn from service in June 1983, and Canada's last KL-7-encrypted message was sent on June 30, 1983, "after 27 years of service."

The successor to the KL-7 was the KL-51, an off-line, paper tape encryption system that used digital electronics instead of rotors.

A set of KL-7 rotors

22.2 Notes

^ Britannica (2005). Proc (2005) differs, saying that, "*after the Walker family spy ring was exposed in the mid-1980s (1985)...immediately, all KL-7's were withdrawn from service*".

22.3   See also

- NSA encryption systems
- Typex

22.4   References

[1] Jerry Proc's page on the KL-7

[2] Method and apparatus for cryptography

22.5   Sources

- Jerry Proc's page on the KL-7, retrieved 2012-08-28.
- NSA Crypto Almanac 50th Anniversary - The development of the AFSAM-7, retrieved 27 February 2011.
- Technical details and history of the TSEC/KL-7, from Dirk Rijmenants' Cipher Machines & Cryptology, retrieved 27 February 2011.
- Patent for Rotor Re-entry by Albert W Small, filed 1944 from Free Patents On-line, retrieved 27 February 2011.
- "Cryptology", Encyclopædia Britannica. Retrieved 22 June 2005 from Encyclopædia Britannica Online .
- Card attached to KL-51 on display at the National Cryptologic Museum, 2005.

22.6   External links

- TSEC/KL-7 with detailed information and many images on the Crypto Museum website
- Accurate TSEC/KL-7 Simulator (Windows), on Dirk Rijmenants' Cipher Machines & Cryptology

Chapter 23

KOI-18

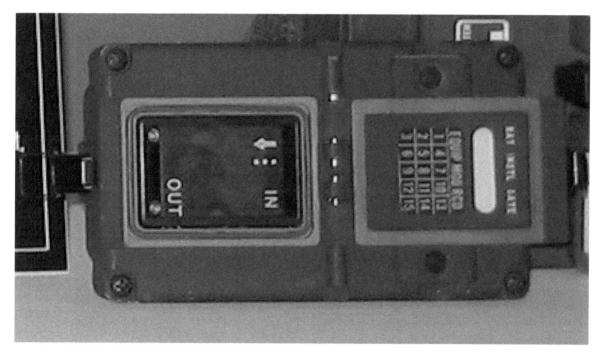

A KOI-18 on display at the National Cryptologic Museum.

The **KOI-18** is a hand-held paper tape reader developed by the U.S. National Security Agency as a fill device for loading cryptographic keys, or "crypto variables," into security devices, such as encryption systems. It can read 8-level paper or PET tape, which is manually pulled through the reader slot by the operator. It is battery powered and has no internal storage, so it can load keys of different lengths, including the 128-bit keys used by more modern systems. The KOI-18 can also be used to load keys into other fill devices that do have internal storage, such as the KYK-13 and AN/CYZ-10. The KOI-18 only supports the DS-102 interface.

A similar device was developed by Prof. Jean-Daniel Nicoud for the Smaky 4 in 1975.[1][2]

23.1 References

[1] CORE 3.1, Computer History Museum, February 2002

[2] Smaky.ch

- US patent 6859537, Houlberg, Christian L.; Borgen, Gary S., "Non-volatile memory for use with an encryption device", issued 2005-02-22

23.2   External links

- KOI-18 diagram

Chapter 24

KOV-14

The **KOV-14 Fortezza Plus** is a US National Security Agency-approved PC card which provides encryption functions and key storage to the Secure Terminal Equipment and other devices.[1] It is a tamper-resistant module based on the Mykotronx Krypton chip, including all of the cryptographic functionality of the original Fortezza card plus the Type 1 algorithms/protocols BATON and Firefly, the SDNS signature algorithm, and the STU-III protocol. It was developed by Mykotronx as part of the NSA's MISSI program. As of 2008, the KOV-14 is beginning to be phased out and replaced by the backwards compatible KSV-21 PC card. [2]

24.1 References

[1] "Department of Defense Awards Enhanced Crypto Card Development Contract to SafeNet". *Business Wire*. 2005-03-14. Retrieved 2009-12-21.

[2] Information Technology Department of the National Nuclear Security Administration. "Solicitation DE-AI52-08NA28817". DoE Industry Interactive Procurement System. Retrieved 2009-12-21.

Chapter 25

KOV-21

The **KOV-21** is a cryptographic PC card module developed under the auspices of the U.S. National Security Agency and manufactured by Sypris Electronics LLC. It is intended to be the cryptographic engine for next generation key management devices, such as the AN/PYQ-10 key loader, as part of the U.S. Government's Cryptographic Modernization Initiative. Sypris was awarded a contract for production of KOV-21 units in November, 2007.

Chapter 26

KSD-64

KSD-64 "Crypto-ignition keys" on display at the National Cryptologic Museum in 2005

The **KSD-64[A] Crypto Ignition Key (CIK)** is an NSA-developed EEPROM chip packed in a plastic case that looks like a toy key. The model number is due to its storage capacity — 64 kilo bits (65,536 bits), enough to store multiple encryption keys. Most frequently it is used in key-splitting applications: either the encryption device or the **KSD-64** alone is worthless, but together they can be used to make encrypted connections. Less often, it is used alone as a fill device for transfer of key material, as for the initial seed key loading of an STU-III secure phone.

Newer systems, such as the Secure Terminal Equipment, use the Fortezza PC card as a security token instead of the KSD-64.

26.1 External links

- Article on STU-III and CIK by Jerry Proc

Chapter 27

KSV-21

The **KSV-21 Enhanced Crypto Card** is a US National Security Agency-approved PC card that provides Type 1 encryption functions and key storage to the STE secure telephones and other devices.

The KSV-21 was originally built by SafeNet but has since been purchased by Raytheon [1] as a tamper-resistant reprogrammable module and is backwards compatible with the KOV-14 Fortezza Plus card. It adds features including support for SCIP, Enhanced Firefly and NSA's 21st century Key Management Initiative. It can perform Type 1 encryption and hash operations at 80 Mbit/s. As of 2008, the KOV-14 is beginning to be phased out and replaced by the KSV-21.[2]

The US version is certified to protect classified data through the Top Secret/SCI level as well as unclassified sensitive information. Versions are available for use with other nations, including:

- Canadian national (KSV-22)

- Combined Communications Electronics Board (CCEB) (KSV-30)

- NATO (KSV-40)

- Coalition Partners (SSV-50)

Prices range from $900 for single units to under $400/each in multi-thousand lot quantities as of 2008.[3]

As of February 2012, the KSV-21 and several related cards had been placed on "end -of-life" status by SafeNet.[4]

27.1   References

[1] *http://www.raytheon.com/capabilities/products/ksv21/index.html". Missing or empty |title= (help);*

[2] Information Technology Department of the National Nuclear Security Administration. "Solicitation DE-AI52-08NA28817". DoE Industry Interactive Procurement System. Retrieved 2009-12-21.

[3] "KSV-21_order_07.pdf" (PDF).

[4] http://www.safenet-inc.com/uploadedFiles/About_SafeNet/Resource_Library/Resource_Items/Other_Docs_EDP/SafeNet_ECC_EOL_Letter.pdf

27.2   External links

- "Voice: Enhanced Crypto Card KSV-21". SafeNet. Retrieved 2009-12-21.

Chapter 28

KW-26

An array of KW-26s

The **TSEC/KW-26**, code named **ROMULUS**, (in 1966 the machine based encryption system was not code-named "Romulus," rather the code-name was "Orion," at least in the US Army's variant) was an encryption system used by the U.S. Government and, later, by NATO countries. It was developed in the 1950s by the National Security Agency (NSA) to secure fixed teleprinter circuits that operated 24 hours a day. It used vacuum tubes and magnetic core logic, replacing older systems, like SIGABA and the British 5-UCO, that used rotors and electromechanical relays.

A KW-26 system (transmitter or receiver) contained over 800 cores and approximately 50 vacuum-tube driver circuits, occupying slightly more than one half of a standard 19-inch rack. Most of the space in the rack and most of the 1 kW input power were required for the special-purpose vacuum tube circuits needed to provide compatibility with multiple input and output circuit configurations. The military services' requirements for numerous modes and speeds significantly increased costs and delayed delivery. NSA says it is doubtful that more than three or four of the possible configurations were ever used.

The KW-26 used an NSA-developed encryption algorithm based on shift registers. The algorithm produced a continuous stream of bits that were xored with the five bit Baudot teleprinter code to produce ciphertext on the transmitting end and plaintext on the receiving end. In NSA terminology, this stream of bits is called the key. The information needed to initialize the algorithm, what most cryptographers today would call the key, NSA calls a **cryptovariable**. Typically each KW-26 was given a new cryptovariable once a day.

NSA designed a common fill device (CFD), for loading the cryptovariable. It used a Remington Rand (UNIVAC) format punched card (45 columns, round holes). The operator inserted the daily key card into the CFD and closed the door securely, locking the card in place. Decks of cards were created by NSA and sent by courier. The cards were strictly accounted for.

Because the KW-26 used a stream cipher, if the same key card was ever used twice, the encryption could be broken. To prevent re-use, the card was automatically cut in half upon reopening the CFD. As the units aged, the card reader contacts became less dependable, and operators resorted to various tricks, such as hitting the card reader cover with a screwdriver, to get them to work properly. Card readers were cleaned and the spring loading of the contacts checked as part of the routine maintenance of the device.

Because the KW-26 sent a continuous stream of bits, it offered traffic-flow security. Someone intercepting the ciphertext stream had no way to judge how many real messages were being sent, making traffic analysis impossible. One problem with the KW-26 was the need to keep the receiver and transmitter units synchronized. The crystal controlled clock in the KW-26 was capable of keeping both ends of the circuit in sync for many hours, even when physical contact was lost between the sending and receiving units. This capability made the KW-26 ideally suited for use on unreliable HF radio circuits. However, when the units did get out of sync, a new key card had to be inserted at each end. The benefit of traffic-flow security was lost each time new cards were inserted. In practice, operational protocol led to the cards being replaced more often than was desirable to maintain maximum security of the circuit. This was especially so on radio circuits, where operators often changed the cards many times each day in response to a loss of radio connectivity. In any case, it was necessary to change the cards at least once per day to prevent the cypher pattern from repeating.

Early KW-26 units protected the **CRITICOMM** network, used to protect communications circuits used to coordinate signals intelligence gathering. The initial production order for this application, awarded to Burroughs in 1957, was for 1500 units. Other services demanded KW-26's and some 14000 units were eventually built, beginning in the early 1960s, for the U.S. Navy, Army, Air Force, Defense Communications Agency, State Department and the CIA. It was provided to U.S. allies as well.

When the USS Pueblo was captured by North Korea in 1968, KW-26's were on board. In response, the NSA had modifications made to other units in the field, presumably changing the crypto algorithm in some way, perhaps by changing the shift register feedback taps. Starting in the mid-1980s, the KW-26 system was decommissioned by NSA, being replaced by the more advanced solid-state data encryptor, TSEC/KG-84.

28.1   See also

- NSA encryption systems

28.2   External links

- KW-26 history page
- NSA brochure on KW-26 history

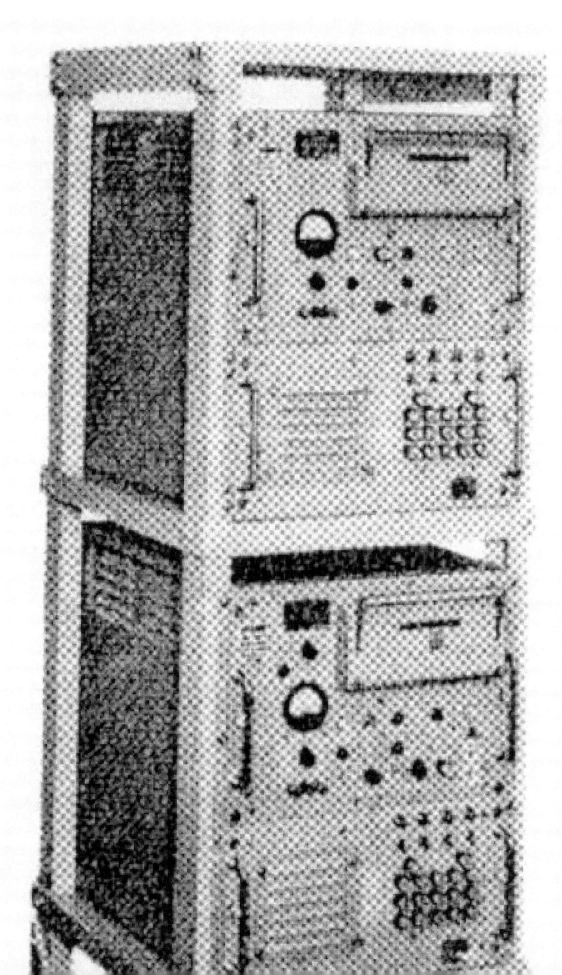

Chapter 29

KW-37

The **KW-37**, code named **JASON**, was an encryption system developed In the 1950s by the U.S. National Security Agency to protect **fleet broadcasts** of the U.S. Navy. Naval doctrine calls for warships at sea to maintain radio silence to the maximum extent possible to prevent ships from being located by potential adversaries using radio direction finding. To allow ships to receive messages and orders, the navy broadcast a continuous stream of information, originally in Morse code and later using radioteletype. Messages were included in this stream as needed and could be for individual ships, battle groups or the fleet as a whole. Each ship's radio room would monitor the broadcast and decode and forward those messages directed at her to the appropriate officer. The KW-37 was designed to automate this process. It consisted of two major components, the **KWR-37** receive unit and the **KWT-37** transmit unit. Each ship had a complement of KWR-37 receivers (usually at least two) that decrypted the fleet broadcast and fed the output to teleprinter machines. KWT-37's were typically located at shore facilities, where high power transmitters were located.

The KWR-37 weighed 100 pounds (45 kg) and contained some 500 subminiature vacuum tubes, whose leads were soldered to printed circuit boards. Each flip-flop in the KW-37 required three tubes, placing an upper bound on the total number of stages in any shift registers used at 166. Squeezing so much logic in such a small and rugged package was quite a feat in the 1950s.

Each KWT-37 filled an entire relay rack with five stacked modules. A precision time reference occupied the bottom, three key generators (stream cyphers in civilian parlance) occupied the middle and an alarm panel occupied the top position. The outputs of the three key generators were combined in a voting circuit. If one of the units' output did not match the other two, an alarm was sounded and the output from the two units that did agree continued to be used.

Each KWR-37 and each key generator in the KWT-37 had a common fill device (CFD) for loading keys (or as NSA calls them **cryptovariables**). The CFDs were similar to that first used in the KW-26, accepting punched cards in Remington Rand format. The key was changed every day at 0000 hours GMT. The receivers were synchronized to the transmitter at that time. If a receiver ever got out of sync, say due to a power failure, an operator had to set the current hour and minute on dials on the front panel. The KWR-37 would then "fast forward" through its key stream sequence until synchronization was re-established.

Large numbers of fleet broadcast key cards had to be produced and distributed to every navy ship and many shore installations on a monthly basis, so many people had access to them. While the key cards were strictly accounted for, they were easy to copy. This proved to be a fatal weakness.

KWR-37s fell into North Korean hands when the USS Pueblo was captured in 1968. New keying material was issued to ships throughout the world to limit the ongoing damage. In 1985 it was revealed that the Walker spy ring had been selling key lists and cards to the Soviet Union for decades. KW-37 systems were taken out of service by the early 1990s.

The received input to the KW(R)−37 was in the form of a multiple broadcast (multicast) signal, consisting of many channels condensed into one tone pack which was deciphered at one stage by the KW(R)−37 and then the output was sent to several KG-14's which further deciphered the then split signals into each channel of the fleet broadcast. The KG-14 also received its timing signal from the KW(R)−37; if the 37 was out of sync, all the 14's were fall out of sync as well. Each KG-14 could process one channel of the tone pack; most fleet units had six KG-14's, larger units even more.

29.1 Experiences operating the KWR-37

Typically, fleet units utilizing the KWR-37 units were outfitted with two devices for redundancy. Should one unit fail, the other one would already be online and patches via a high level, 60-milliamp patch panel would quickly be changed around so that the current offline unit could be changed over to online status at a moment's notice, to ensure that there was no interruption of message traffic. Later in their life, when KWR-37 units were aged and worn, sometimes the circuit cards inside had to be reseated with a rubber mallet which helped ensure the cards were reseated properly. Other problems with the KWR-37's were related to the startup times. Fleet radiomen, and those stationed in the shore transmitting stations, had to listen to an HF signal for coordinated universal time. Radiomen called this broadcast the "time tick," which gave them a sharp tone, signalling them to press the restart button so that the unit could then start up for "new day" or otherwise known as "HJ's" by the radiomen. This took place after the new day's crypto keylist card was properly inserted into the "crib" or the card reader by securing it onto pins and then firmly closing the card access door and then locking it with a key. Once the unit(s) were restarted, the key was placed back in the safe using two-person integrity (TPI) which was stringently enforced following the Walker spy investigation. In the early nineties when the KWR-37 units were retired from the navy and replaced by the more reliable and modern KWR-46's, fleet Radiomen breathed a sigh of relief because the KWR-37 units were often unreliable and would occasionally fall out of synchronization timing, resulting in a loss of broadcast messages from the various fleet channels.

29.2 Sources

- The KWR-37 On-line Crypto Receiver — Jerry Proc: "Crypto Machines", HMCS *Haida* National Historic Site (2010).

Experiences operating the KWR-37 - a personal account from a retired US Navy fleet Radioman

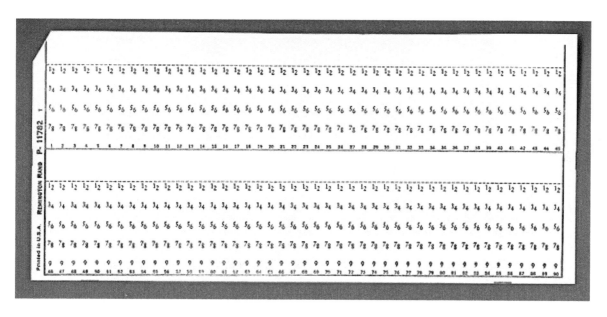

Remington Rand format punch card similar to the type used by NSA to distribute keys.

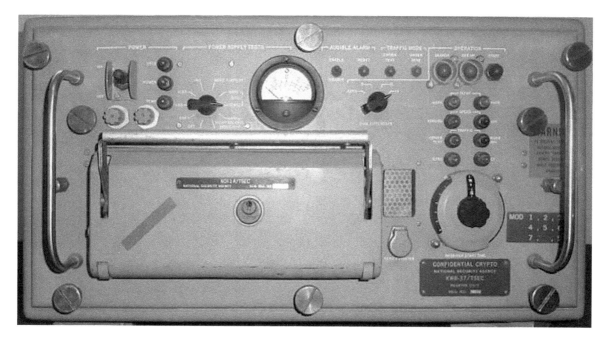

TSEC KW-37 Receiver on display at the Naval History museum at La Spezia, Italy.

Chapter 30

KY-3

This article is about the telephone system. For other uses, see KY 3 (disambiguation).

The **KY-3** (TSEC/KY-3) is a secure telephone system developed by the U.S. National Security Agency in the early 1960s. The "TSEC" prefix to the model number indicates NSA's Telecommunications Security nomenclature system.

According to information on display in 2002 at the NSA's National Cryptologic Museum, the KY-3 provided high fidelity secure voice over special wideband circuits known as "4-wire dedicated drops". It was used by executives, diplomats, military leaders and the intelligence community. Some 2500 units were produced between 1965 and 1967 and it was one of the first telecommunication security devices to use transistors packaged into functional modules. The unit was packaged in a grey relay rack cabinet. The KY-3 was replaced by the STU-I and STU-II.

30.1 External links

- Delusion.org - National Cryptologic Museum pictures

30.2 See also

- STU-III
- Secure Terminal Equipment
- SCIP

Chapter 31

KY-57

For the highway, see Kentucky Route 57.

The **Speech Security Equipment (VINSON), TSEC/KY-57**, is a portable, tactical cryptographic device in the

A KY-57 on display at the National Cryptologic Museum.

VINSON family, designed to provide voice encryption for a range of military communication devices such as radio or telephone.

The KY-57 can accept signal fades of up to 12 seconds without losing synchronization with the transmitting station. There are storage positions for 6 keys. Keys 1 to 5 are traffic encryption keys (TEK). Key 6 is a key encryption key (KEK) used for over the air rekeying (OTAR) of the other 5 keys. Key 6 must be loaded manually using a fill device such as the AN/CYZ-10.

31.1   See also

- NSA encryption systems

- FNBDT

- ANDVT

- SINCGARS

- AN/PRC-77

31.2   External links

- A description of the KY-57

- Another description with a photo

Chapter 32

KY-58

The VINSON **KY-58** is a secure voice module primarily used to encrypt radio communication to and from military aircraft and other tactical vehicles. It is employed by U.S. Military Joint Services, NATO and some law enforcement agencies. It is designed to operate over bandwidth-restricted circuits such as UHF and VHF satellite access and wideband switched telephone systems. It uses the 16 kbit/s continuously variable slope delta modulation (CVSD). The system was initially fielded as a replacement for the KG-36 and KG-34. The unit fits in a five inch cube and weighs about 5 pounds. Production ended in 1993.

32.1 See also

- KY-57
- KY-68

32.2 External links

- KY-58 (Vinson) by Jerry Proc
- Interactive KY-58 graphics explaining the controls

Chapter 33

KY-68

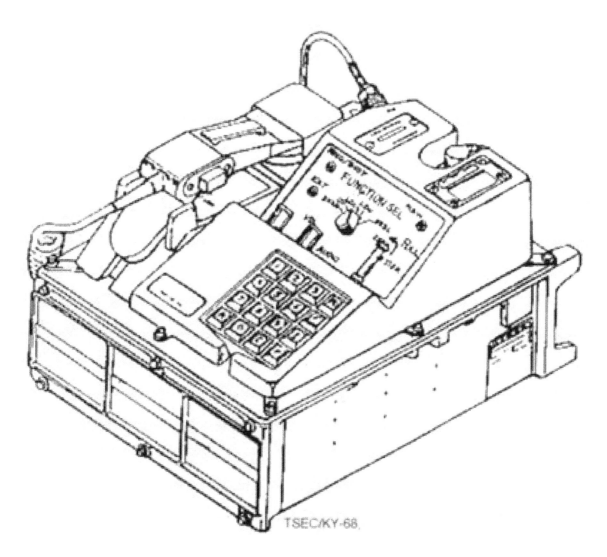

TSEC/KY68 Basic Unit

TSEC/KY-68 DSVT, commonly known as **Digital Subscriber Voice Terminal**, is a US military ruggedized, full- or half-duplex tactical telephone system with a built-in encryption/decryption module for secure traffic.

It transmits voice and data at 16 or 32 kbit/s, converting voice to a digital signal. The KY-68 can operate via civilian and military switches in either encrypted or un-encrypted mode, or point-to-point (encrypted mode only).

Although used primarily for secure communications, the KY-68 can also transmit to a Digital Non-secure Voice Terminal (DNVT). A local switch warns the KY-68 user with a tone signal when initiating communication with a non-secure terminal.

The KY-68 is keyed using an Electronic Transfer Device, typically either a KYK-13 or AN/CYZ-10.

An almost identical office version (KY-78) features the same electronics as the KY-68, but has an exterior casing composed of lighter materials.

The KY-68 and KY-78 are approved for use with SECRET-classified information, and despite the KY-78 being compromised in the early 1990s, both versions remain in use.

33.1   See also

- KY-57
- KY-58

33.2   External links

- Jerry Proc's page on the KY-68
- The Signal Leader's Guide — Field Manual 11-43

Chapter 34

KYK-13

KYK-13 on display at the National Cryptologic Museum.

The **KYK-13 Electronic Transfer Device** is a common fill device designed by the United States National Security Agency for the transfer and loading of cryptographic keys with their corresponding check word. The KYK-13 is battery powered and uses the DS-102 protocol for key transfer. Its National Stock Number is 5810-01-026-9618.

Even though the KYK-13 is several decades old and was supposed to have been obsoleted by the AN/CYZ-10 Data Transfer Device, it is still widely used because of its simplicity and reliability.[1] A simpler device than the CYZ-10, the KIK-30 "Really Simple Key loader" (RASKL) is now planned to replace the KYK-13s, with up to $200 million budgeted to procure them in quantity.[2][3]

34.1   Components

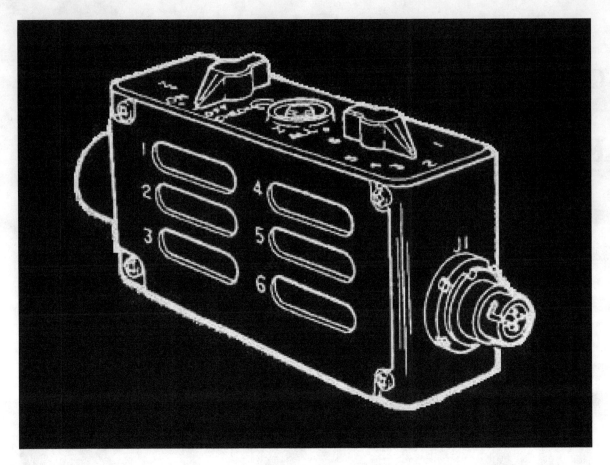

KYK-13

- P1 and J1 Connectors - Electrically the same connection. Used to connect to a fill cable, COMSEC device, KOI-18, KYX-15, or another KYK-13, or AN/CYZ-10.

- Battery Compartment - Holds battery which powers KYK-13.

- Mode Switch - Three position rotary switch used to select operation modes.

   - "Z" - Used to zeroize selected keys.

   - ON - Used to fill and transfer keys.

   - OFF CHECK - Used to conduct parity checks.

- Parity Lamp - Blinks when parity is checked or fill is transferred.

- Initiate Push button - Push this button when loading or zeroizing the KYK-13.

- Address Select Switch - Seven position rotary switch.

   - "Z" ALL - Zeroizes all 6 storage registers when mode switch is set to "Z".

   - 1 THROUGH 6 - Six storage registers for storing keys in KYK-13.

34.2   References

[1]

[2] KIK-30 The First Modernized KYK-13 Replacement

[3] http://defensesystems.com/articles/2009/11/12/dod-cryptographic-key.aspx

Chapter 35

Navajo I

The **Navajo I** is a secure telephone built into a briefcase that was developed by the U.S. National Security Agency. According to information on display in 2002 at the NSA's National Cryptologic Museum, 110 units were built in the 1980s for use by senior government officials when traveling. It uses the linear predictive coding algorithm LPC-10 at 2.4 kilobits/second.

The name is most likely a reference to the Navajo code talkers of World War II.

35.1 Source

Display labels from .

35.2 See also

- STU-II
- SCIP

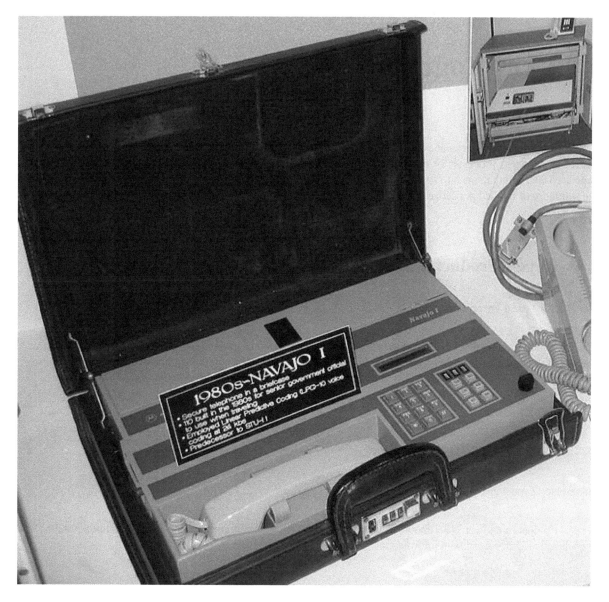

Navajo I secure telephone

Chapter 36

NSA cryptography

The vast majority of the National Security Agency's work on encryption is classified, but from time to time NSA participates in standards processes or otherwise publishes information about its cryptographic algorithms. The NSA has categorized encryption items into four product types, and algorithms into two suites. The following is a brief and incomplete summary of public knowledge about NSA algorithms and protocols.

36.1   Type 1 Product

Main article: Type 1 encryption

A Type 1 Product refers to an NSA endorsed classified or controlled cryptographic item for classified or sensitive U.S. government information, including cryptographic equipment, assembly or component classified or certified by NSA for encrypting and decrypting classified and sensitive national security information when appropriately keyed.[1]

36.2   Type 2 Product

Main article: Type 2 encryption

A Type 2 Product refers to an NSA endorsed unclassified cryptographic equipment, assemblies or components for sensitive but unclassified U.S. government information.

36.3   Type 3 Product

Main article: Type 3 encryption

Unclassified cryptographic equipment, assembly, or component used, when appropriately keyed, for encrypting or decrypting unclassified sensitive U.S. Government or commercial information, and to protect systems requiring protection mechanisms consistent with standard commercial practices. A Type 3 Algorithm refers to NIST endorsed algorithms, registered and FIPS published, for sensitive but unclassified U.S. government and commercial information.

36.4 Type 4 Product

Main article: Type 4 encryption

A Type 4 Algorithm refers to algorithms that are registered by the NIST but are not FIPS published. Unevaluated commercial cryptographic equipment, assemblies, or components that are neither NSA nor NIST certify for any Government usage.

36.5 Algorithm Suites

36.5.1 Suite A

Main article: NSA Suite A Cryptography

A set of NSA unpublished algorithms that is intended for highly sensitive communication and critical authentication systems.

36.5.2 Suite B

Main article: NSA Suite B Cryptography

A set of NSA endorsed cryptographic algorithms for use as an interoperable cryptographic base for both unclassified information and most classified information. Suite B was announced on 16 February 2005.

36.5.3 Quantum resistant suite

In August, 2015, NSA announced that it is planning to transition "in the not distant future" to a new cipher suite that is resistant to quantum attacks. "Unfortunately, the growth of elliptic curve use has bumped up against the fact of continued progress in the research on quantum computing, necessitating a re-evaluation of our cryptographic strategy." NSA advised: "For those partners and vendors that have not yet made the transition to Suite B algorithms, we recommend not making a significant expenditure to do so at this point but instead to prepare for the upcoming quantum resistant algorithm transition."[3]

36.6 See also

- NSA encryption systems
- Speck and Simon, light-weight block ciphers, published by NSA in 2013

36.7 References

[1] "National Information Assurance Glossary"; CNSS Instruction No. 4009 National Information Assurance Glossary

[2] ViaSat Programmable Scalable Information Assurance Model (PSIAM)

[3] https://www.nsa.gov/ia/programs/suiteb_cryptography/index.shtml

Chapter 37

Over the Air Rekeying

Over the Air Rekeying (**OTAR**) is the common name for the method of changing or updating encryption keys in a two-way radio system over the radio channel ("over the air"). It is also referred to as Over-the-Air Transfer (OTAT), depending on the specific type and use of key being changed. Although the acronym refers specifically to radio transmission means, the technology is also employed via land line and cable.

Many of the newer NSA cryptographic systems that use a 128-bit electronic key, such as the ANDVT, KY-58, KG-84A/C, and KY-75, are capable of obtaining new or updated keys via the circuit they protect or other secure communications circuits. This process is known as over-the-air rekey (OTAR) or over-the-air transfer (OTAT). The use of OTAR/OTAT drastically reduces the distribution of physical keying material and the physical process of loading cryptographic devices with key tapes. A station may have nothing to do with actual physical key changeovers on a day-to-day basis. The electronic key would normally come from the Net Control Station (NCS). The added feature of OTAT is that the key can be extracted from an OTAT-capable cryptographic system using a fill device, such as the KYK-13 or KYX-15/KYX-15A. The key is then loaded into another cryptographic system as needed.

OTAR technology and methods were operationally introduced to the US Department of Defense via the Navy in 1991 through 1993. Lieutenant Commander David D. Winters, an American naval officer stationed in London, early recognized the necessity for these advances and personally oversaw development and deployment of the innovative procedures required. His methods were quickly adopted and spread Navy wide. Shortly thereafter, when joint US forces became heavily tasked in the Middle-East and Eastern Europe, Commander Winters was dispatched to the combat zones where he introduced these same capabilities to the Air force, Army, and Allied forces.

This revolutionized US and associated military telecommunications security by eliminating the previous requirements for risky, expensive wide-spread distribution of paper code keys. It thereby extinguished vulnerability to physical theft and loss previously exploited by the infamous Jonathan Walker spy ring.[1] Elimination of this vulnerability, although little appreciated outside the security community at the time, was an innovation of inestimable impact.

Winters's contributions were quietly recognized and mentioned in official history,[2] military awards and by his election in 2003 to membership in the elite British Special Forces Club.[3]

37.1   References

[1] See John Anthony Walker.

[2] "OPERATION PROVIDE COMFORT, A Communications Perspective, *published by the United States European Command Directorate of Command, Control, and Communications, June 4, 1993.*

[3] See Special Forces Club

Chapter 38

Secure Communications Interoperability Protocol

The **Secure Communications Interoperability Protocol** (**SCIP**) is a multinational standard for secure voice and data communication. SCIP derived from the US Government **Future Narrowband Digital Terminal** (**FNBDT**) project after the US offered to share details of FNBDT with other nations in 2003.[1] SCIP supports a number of different modes, including national and multinational modes which employ different cryptography. Many nations and industries develop SCIP devices to support the multinational and national modes of SCIP.

SCIP has to operate over the wide variety of communications systems, including commercial land line telephone, military radios, communication satellites, Voice over IP and the several different cellular telephone standards. Therefore it was designed to make no assumptions about the underlying channel other than a minimum bandwidth of 2400 Hz. It is similar to a dial-up modem in that once a connection is made, two SCIP phones first negotiate the parameters they need and then communicate in the best way possible.

US SCIP or FNBDT systems were used since 2001, beginning with the CONDOR secure cell phone. The standard is designed to cover wideband as well as narrowband voice and data security.

SCIP was designed by the Department of Defense Digital Voice Processor Consortium (DDVPC) in cooperation with the U.S. National Security Agency and is intended to solve problems with earlier NSA encryption systems for voice, including STU-III and Secure Terminal Equipment (STE) which made assumptions about the underlying communication systems that prevented interoperability with more modern wireless systems. STE sets can be upgraded to work with SCIP, but STU-III cannot. This has led to some resistance since various government agencies already own over 350,000 STU-III telephones at a cost of several thousand dollars each.

There are several components to the SCIP standard: key management, voice compression, encryption and a signalling plan for voice, data and multimedia applications.

38.1   Key Management (120)

To set up a secure call, a new Traffic Encryption Key (**TEK**) must be negotiated. For Type 1 security (classified calls), the SCIP signalling plan uses an enhanced FIREFLY messaging system for key exchange. FIREFLY is an NSA key management system based on public key cryptography. At least one commercial grade implementation uses Diffie-Hellman key exchange.

STEs use security tokens to limit use of the secure voice capability to authorized users while other SCIP devices only require a PIN code, 7 digits for Type 1 security, 4 digits for unclassified.

38.2   Voice compression using Voice Coders (vocoders)

SCIP can work with a variety of vocoders. The standard requires, as a minimum, support for the mixed-excitation linear prediction (MELP) coder, an enhanced MELP algorithm known as MELPe, with additional preprocessing, analyzer and synthesizer capabilities for improved intelligibility and noise robustness. The old MELP and the new MELPe are interoperable and both operate at 2400 bit/s, sending a 54 bit data frame every 22.5 milliseconds but the MELPe has optional additional rates of 1200 bit/s and 600 bit/s.

2400 bit/s MELPe is the only mandatory voice coder required for SCIP. Other voice coders can be supported in terminals. These can be used if all terminals involved in the call support the same coder (agreed during the negotiation stage of call setup) and the network can support the required throughput. G.729D is the most widely supported non-mandatory voice coder in SCIP terminals as it offers a good compromise between higher voice quality without dramatically increasing the required throughput.

38.3   Encryption (SCIP 23x)

The security used by the multinational and national modes of SCIP is defined by the SCIP 23x family of documents. SCIP 231 defines AES based cryptography which can be used multinationally. SCIP 232 defines an alternate multinational cryptographic solution. Several nations have defined, or are defining, their own national security modes for SCIP.

38.4   US National Mode (SCIP 230)

SCIP 230 defines the cryptography of the US national mode of SCIP. The rest of this section refers to SCIP 230. For security, SCIP uses a block cipher operating in counter mode. A new Traffic Encryption Key (**TEK**) is negotiated for each call. The block cipher is fed a 64-bit state vector (**SV**) as input. If the cipher's block size is longer than 64 bits, a fixed filler is added. The output from the block cipher is xored with the MELP data frames to create the cipher text that is then transmitted.

The low-order two bits of the state vector are reserved for applications where the data frame is longer than the block cipher output. The next 42 bits are the counter. Four bits are used to represent the transmission mode. This allows more than one mode, e.g. voice and data, to operate at the same time with the same TEK. The high-order 16 bits are a sender ID. This allows multiple senders on a single channel to all use the same TEK. Note that since overall SCIP encryption is effectively a stream cipher, it is essential that the same state vector value never be used twice for a given TEK. At MELP data rates, a 42-bit counter allows a call over three thousand years long before the encryption repeats.

For Type 1 security, SCIP uses BATON, a 128-bit block design. With this or other 128-bit ciphers, such as AES, SCIP specifies that two data frames are encrypted with each cipher output bloc, the first beginning at bit 1, the second at bit 57 (i.e. the next byte boundary). At least one commercial grade implementation uses the Triple DES cipher.

38.5   Signalling plan (210)

The SCIP signalling plan is common to all national and multinational modes of SCIP. SCIP has two mandatory types of transmission. The mandatory data service uses an ARQ protocol with forward error correction (FEC) to ensure reliable transmission. The receiving station acknowledges accurate receipt of data blocks and can ask for a block to be re-transmitted, if necessary. For voice, SCIP simply sends a stream of voice data frames (typically MELPe frames, but possibly G.729D or another codec if that has been negotiated between the terminals). To save power on voice calls, SCIP stops sending if there is no speech input. A synchronization block is sent roughly twice a second in place of a data frame. The low order 14 bits of the encryption counter are sent with every sync block. The 14 bits are enough to cover a fade out of more than six minutes. Part of the rest of the state vector are sent as well so that with receipt of three sync blocks, the entire state vector is recovered. This handles longer fades and allows a station with the proper TEK to join a multi station net and be synchronized within 1.5 seconds.

38.6 Availability

As of March 2011 a range of SCIP documents, including the SCIP-210 signalling standard, are publicly available from the IAD website.[2]

Prior to this, SCIP specifications were not widely diffused or easily accessible. This made the protocol for government use rather "opaque" outside governments or defense industries. No public implementation of the Type 1 security and transport protocols are available, precluding its security from being publicly verified.

38.7 See also

- Secure voice
- ZRTP
- MELP
- MELPe
- CVSD
- CELP
- LPC-10e
- FS1015
- FS1016
- ANDVT
- Secure Terminal Equipment
- L-3 Omni/Omni xi
- Sectéra secure voice family

38.8 Notes

[1] Introduction to FNBDT by NC3A discusses the prospects for FNBDT for NATO in 2003

[2] SCIP-related documents are made available through the Information Assurance Directorate web site. Documents can be retrieved by typing "SCIP" into the IAD SecurePhone document search web page

38.9 References

- *Securing the Wireless Environment (FNBDT)*, briefing available from http://wireless.securephone.net/
- *Secure Communications Interoperability Protocols, SCIP*, HFIA briefing available at http://www.hfindustry.com/Sept05/Sept2005_Presentations/HFIAbriefing.ppt

Chapter 39

Secure DTD2000 System

The KIK-20 **Secure DTD2000 System** (SDS) is a key fill device developed by Sypris Electronics, Florida, US, under the auspices of the U.S. National Security Agency. It, along with the AN/PYQ-10, is intended to eventually replace the AN/CYZ-10 key fill device, along with older units still in service, and can support a wide variety of cryptographic devices and key types.

The SDS is roughly the same size as the CYZ-10 — 7.4" (188mm) x 4.25" (108) x 1.8" (46mm) — and weighs less than 2.5 lbs (1.1 kg). It uses an XScale processor running at 300 MHz under the Microsoft Windows CE operating system. Cryptographic functions are performed by an internal KOV-21 crypto PC Card. The SDS includes 64 MB of RAM, 32 MB of flash read-only memory, a QWERTY keyboard, half-VGA color display, and a USB port. It also has a 6-pin connector for cabling to NSA standard fill connectors. The keyboard includes two zeroize buttons. It costs US$3700 each.

39.1 Source

SDS

Chapter 40

SINCGARS

Single Channel Ground and Airborne Radio System (**SINCGARS**) is a Combat Net Radio (CNR) currently used by U.S. and allied military forces. The radios, which handle voice and data communications, are designed to be reliable, secure, and easily maintained. Vehicle-mount, backpack, airborne, and handheld form factors are available.

SINCGARS uses 25 kHz channels in the very high frequency (VHF) FM band, from 30 to 87.975 Megahertz (MHz). It has single-frequency and frequency hopping modes. The frequency-hopping mode hops 111 times a second.

The SINCGARS family has mostly replaced the Vietnam-war-era synthesized single frequency radios (AN/PRC-77 and AN/VRC-12), although it can work with them. The airborne AN/ARC-201 radio is phasing out the older tactical air-to-ground radios (AN/ARC-114 and AN/ARC-131).

Over 570,000 radios have been purchased.[1] There have been several system improvement programs, including the Integrated Communications Security (ICOM) models, which have provided integrated voice and data encryption, the Special Improvement Program (SIP) models, which add additional data modes, and the advanced SIP (ASIP) models, which are less than half the size and weight of ICOM and SIP models and provided enhanced FEC (forward error correction) data modes, RS-232 asynchronous data, Packet Data formats, and direct interfacing to Precision Lightweight GPS Receiver (PLGR) devices providing radio level situational awareness capability.

In 1992, the U.S. Air Force awarded a contract to replace the AN/ARC-188 for communications between Air Force aircraft and Army units.

40.1   Timeline

- November 1983: ITT Corporation (ITT) wins the contract for the first type of radio, for ground troops.

- May 1985: ITT wins the contract for the airborne SINCGARS.

- July 1988: General Dynamics wins a second-source contract for the ground radio.

- April 1989: ITT reaches "Milestone IIIB": full-rate production.

- December 1990: 1st Division is equipped.

- December 1991: General Dynamics wins the "Option 1 Award" for the ground radio.

- March 1992: ITT wins a "Ground and Airborne" award.

- July 1992: Magnavox Electronics Systems Company develops the airborne SINCGARS AN/ARC-222 for the Air Force

- August 1993: General Dynamics achieves full rate production.

- April 1994: ITT and General Dynamics compete for the ground radio.

- May 1994: ITT wins a sole-source contract for the airborne radio.

- 1997: ITT became the sole source supplier of the new half-size RT-1523E radio to the US Army.

- 2006: The RT-1523F/SideHat configuration provides a 2-channel capability.

- July 2009: ITT wins RT-1523G platform development, $363 Million Dollar Contract. Partnered with Thales Communications Inc.

- 2012: Capability Set 14 to provide Universal Network Situational Awareness to help prevent air-to-ground friendly fire incidents.[2]

40.2 Models

40.3 RT-1523 VHF radio configurations

40.4 Ancillary items

- SideHat - The 'SideHat' is a simple radio solution that attaches to existing SINCGARS radio installations, offering rapid, affordable and interoperable wideband network communications for Early Infantry Brigade Combat Team (E-IBCT) deployments and other Soldier radio waveform (SRW) applications.[4]

- SINCGARS Airborne - The AN/ARC-201 System Improvement Program (SIP) airborne radio is a reliable, field-proven voice and data battlespace communications system with networking capabilities.[5]

- Embedded GPS Receiver - The Selective Availability Antispoofing Module (SAASM) technology Embedded GPS Receiver (EGR) installed in the RT-1523(E)-(F) providing a navigation/communication system in support of critical Warfighter capabilities that includes Situational Awareness, Combat ID, Navigation and Timing and Surveying Capabilities.[6]

- GPS FanOut System - Provides six GPS formats from a single GPS source (RT-1523 with integrated SAASM GPS or PLGR/DAGR (Defense Advanced GPS Receiver–AN/PSN-13)).[7]

- VRCU (Vehicle Remote Control Unit) - Designed to be placed anywhere on a vehicle, VRCU is important in large vehicles and those with tight quarters. VRCU allows full control of both single and dual RT-1523 (models E, F, and G) and RT-1702 (models E and F) radios from any location within a vehicle.[8]

- Single ASIP Radio Mount (SARM) is the latest vehicle installation mount developed specifically for RT-1523 or RT-1702 radios. SARM solves space and weight claim issues associated with traditional vehicle installation mounts. SARM operates on 12 or 24 volt allowing installation into any military or civilian vehicle.[9]

40.5 References

[1] Erwin, Sandra I. (February 2007). "Delays in 'joint tactical radio' program cast doubts on future". nationaldefensemagazine. Retrieved 2015-10-12.

[2] Thompson, Edric. "Radio-based combat ID -- for free." *RDECOM*, 2012-10-10. Retrieved 2015-10-12 – Via globalsecurity.org

[3] "SINCGARS RT-1523 VHF Radio Configurations" (PDF-537 KB). *Exelisinc.com*. Exelis Inc. 2013. Retrieved 2015-10-12.

[4] "Exelis - SideHat". *exelisinc.com*. Retrieved 2015-10-12.

[5] "Exelis - SINCGARS Airborne Radio". *exelisinc.com*. Retrieved 2015-10-12.

[6] "Exelis - SINCGARS Embedded GPS Receiver". *exelisinc.com*. Retrieved 2015-10-12.

[7] "Exelis - SINCGARS GPS FanOut System". *exelisinc.com*. Retrieved 2015-10-12.

[8] "Exelis - SINCGARS Vehicle Remote Control Unit (VRCU)". *exelisinc.com*. Retrieved 2015-10-12.

[9] "Exelis - Single ASIP Radio Mount (SARM)". *exelisinc.com*. Retrieved 2015-10-12.

40.6   External links

- RT-1523 VHF Radio Data sheet exelisinc.com (pdf)

- RT-1702 VHF Radio Data sheet exelisinc.com (pdf)

- Single Channel Ground and Airborne Radio System (SINCGARS) www.fas.org

- FISCAL YEAR 1997 COMMAND, CONTROL, COMMUNICATIONS, COMPUTERS, INTELLIGENCE, ELECTRONIC WARFARE AND SENSORS (C4IEWS) PROJECT BOOK monmouth.army.mil

- www.globalsecurity.org - N.b.: development contractor for the ARC-222 was Magnavox in Fort Wayne, Indiana, not Raytheon as stated. See link above

- Summary of the AN/VRC-92F Jane's

- Information on RT-1439 radio prc68.com

A SINCGARS is being operated from within a HMMWV

A Marine Corps 2nd Lt operates a PRC 119 during training in Quantico, Virginia

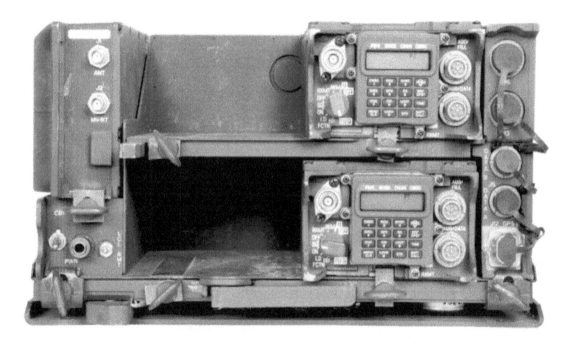

VRC-89, two radios installed

Chapter 41

STU-I

This article is about a secure telephone. For Stu as a common name, see Stuart (disambiguation).
For other uses, see STU (disambiguation).

The **STU-I**, like its successors sometimes known as a "stew phone", was a secure telephone developed by the U.S. National Security Agency for use by senior U.S. government officials in the 1970s.

41.1 See also

- KY-3
- Navajo I
- STU-II
- STU-III
- SCIP

41.2 External links

- Delusion.org - National Cryptologic Museum pictures

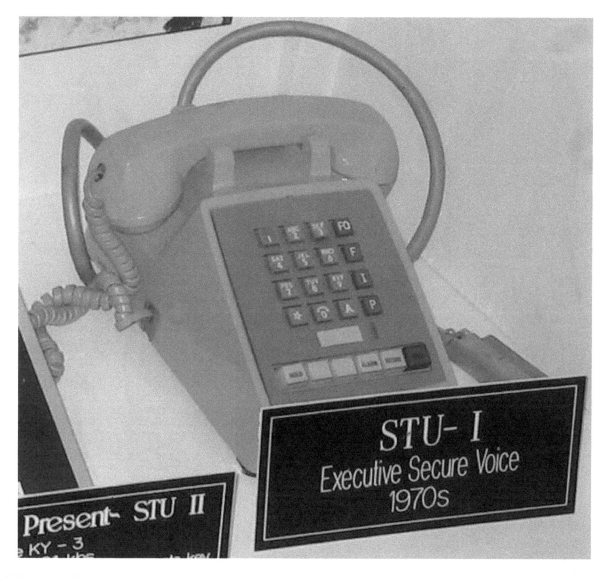

STU-I secure telephone desk set. Electronics were housed in a separate cabinet.

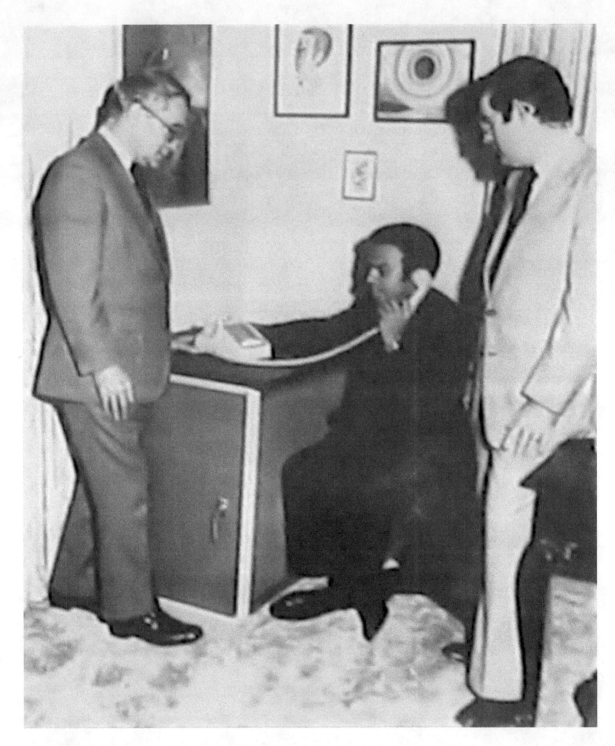

STU-1 cabinet with desk set on top. The person talking is U.N. Ambassador Andrew Young, calling from New York City during the Israel-Egypt peace talks in the Carter administration.

Chapter 42

STU-II

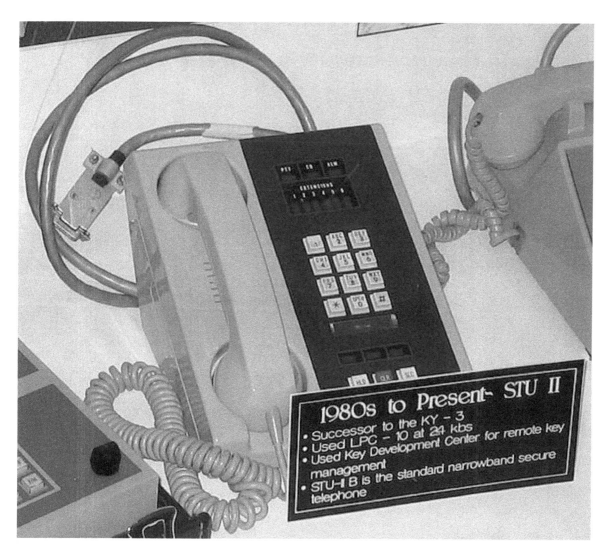

STU-II secure telephone desk set. Electronics were housed in a separate cabinet.

The **STU-II** is a secure telephone developed by the U.S. National Security Agency. It permitted up to six users to have secure communications, on a time-shared (e.g.: rotating) basis. It was made by ITT Defense Communications, Nutley,

New Jersey. An OEM partner was Northern Telecom.

According to information on display in 2005 at the NSA's National Cryptologic Museum, the STU-II was in use from the 1980s to the present. It uses the linear predictive coding algorithm LPC-10 at 2.4 kilobits/second to digitize voice, and the "Key Distribution Center" (KDC) for key management. The display also stated that the STU-II B is the standard narrow band secure telephone.

STU-II replaced the STU-I, KY-3 and the Navajo I. The last was a secure telephone in a briefcase, of which 110 were built in the 1980s for use by senior government officials when traveling. The Navaho I also used LPC-10.

Some 10 000 STU-II units were produced.

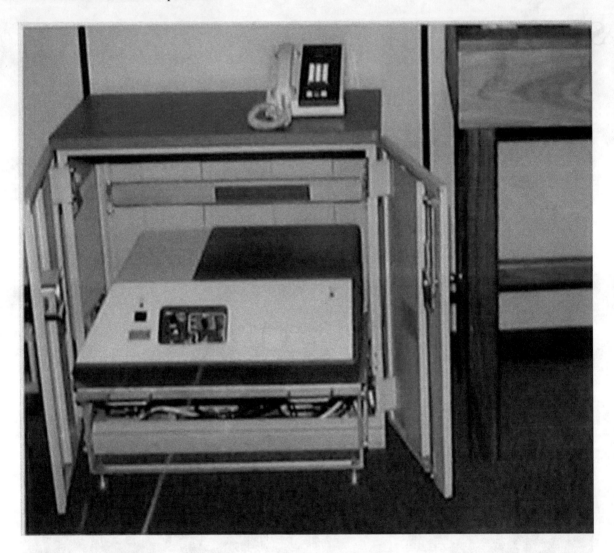

STU-II cabinet with desk set on top.

42.1   External links

- Delusion.org - National Cryptologic Museum pictures

- Pictures of president Reagan using a STU-II phone

42.2　See also

- STU-III
- SCIP

Chapter 43

STU-III

A STU-III secure telephone (AT&T model)

STU-III is a family of secure telephones introduced in 1987 by the NSA for use by the United States government, its contractors, and its allies. STU-III desk units look much like typical office telephones, plug into a standard telephone wall jack and can make calls to any ordinary phone user (with such calls receiving no special protection, however). When a call is placed to another STU-III unit that is properly set up, one caller can ask the other to initiate secure transmission. They then press a button on their telephones and, after a 15 second delay, their call is encrypted to prevent eavesdropping. There are portable and militarized versions and most STU-IIIs contained an internal modem and RS-232 port for data and fax transmission. Vendors were AT&T (later transferred to Lucent Technologies), RCA (Now L-3 Communications, East) and Motorola.

STU-III are no longer in service with the U.S. Government, with the last cryptographic keys for the units expiring on December 31, 2009. It has been replaced by the STE (Secure Terminal Equipment) and other equipment using the more modern Secure Communications Interoperability Protocol (SCIP).[1]

43.1   Versions

- STU-III/Low Cost Terminal (LCT) designed for use in office environment by all types of users. (Motorola Sectel 1500, Lucent Technologies/GD 1100 and 1150)

George W. Bush using a Motorola STU-III immediately after the September 11 attacks

- STU-III/Cellular Telephone (CT) is interoperable with all STU-III versions. Works in all continental US mobile network and in most of the foreign cellular networks.

- STU-III/Allied (A) specialized version of the STU-III/LCT that is compatible with the STU-II. It retains all basic STU-III functions and capabilities and incorporates STU-II BELLFIELD KDC, STU-II net, and STU-II multipoint modes of operation.

- STU-III/Remote Control Interface (R or RCU)

- STU-III/MultiMedia Terminal (MMT)

- STU-III/Inter Working Function (IWF)

- STU-III/Secure Data Device (SDD)

- STU-III/CipherTAC 2000 (CTAC)

43.2   Security

Most STU-III units were built for use with what NSA calls Type 1 encryption. This allows them to protect conversations at all security classification levels up to Top Secret, with the maximum level permitted on a call being the lower clearance level of the two persons talking. At the height of the Commercial COMSEC Endorsement Program, Type 2, 3, and 4 STU-IIIs were manufactured, but they saw little commercial success.

Two major factors in the STU-III's success were the Electronic Key Management System (EKMS) and the use of a removable memory module in a plastic package in the shape of a house key, called a KSD-64A. The EKMS is believed

STU-III secure telephones on display at the National Cryptologic Museum in 2005.

to be one of the first widespread applications of asymmetric cryptography. It greatly reduced the complex logistics and bookkeeping associated with ensuring each encryption device has the right keys and that all keying material is protected and accounted for.

The KSD-64A contains a 64kbit EEPROM chip that can be used to store various types of keying and other information. A new (or zeroized) STU-III must first have a "seed key" installed. This key is shipped from NSA by registered mail or Defense Courier Service. Once the STU-III has its seed key, the user calls an 800-number at NSA to have the seed key converted into an operational key. A list of compromised keys is downloaded to the STU-III at this time. The operational key is supposed to be renewed at least once a year.

The operational key is then split into two components, one of which replaces the information on the KSD-64A, at which point it becomes a Crypto Ignition Key or CIK. When the CIK is removed from the STU-III telephone neither unit is considered classified. Only when the CIK is inserted into the STU-III on which it was created can classified information be received and sent.

When a call "goes secure", the two STU-III's create a unique key that will be used to encrypt just this call. Each unit first makes sure that the other is not using a revoked key and if one has a more up-to-date key revocation list it transmits it to the other. Presumably the revocation lists are protected by a digital signature generated by NSA.

While there have been no reports of STU-III encryption being broken, there have been claims that foreign intelligence services can recognize the lines on which STU-IIIs are installed and that un-encrypted calls on these lines, particularly what was said while waiting for the "go secure" command to complete, have provided valuable information.

43.3   Use

Hundreds of thousands of STU-III sets were produced and many were still in use as of 2004. STU-III replaced earlier voice encryption devices, including the KY-3 (1960s), the STU-I (1970) and the STU-II (1975). The STU-II had some 10,000 users. These, in turn, replaced less secure voice scramblers. Unlike earlier systems, the STU-III's encryption electronics are completely contained in the desk set. The STU-III is no longer in use, having been replaced by the STE (Secure Terminal Equipment) or OMNI, more modern, all digital systems that overcome many of the STU-III's problems, including the 15 second delay.

Operational difficulties in using STU-III phones hindered coordination between the Federal Aviation Administration and NORAD during the September 11, 2001 attacks on New York and Washington. *See* Communication during the September 11 attacks.

STE succeeded STU-III in the 1990s. Similar to STU-III, an STE unit physically resembles an ordinary telephone.

Besides connecting to a regular wall phone jack (Public Switched Telephone Network), the STE was originally designed to be connected to Integrated Services Digital Network (ISDN) lines. As a result, in addition to having secured voice conversations, users can also use an STE unit for classified data and fax transmissions. Transfer rate of an STE is also considerably higher (STU-III: up to 9 kbit/s; STE: up to 128 kbit/s). Lastly, an STE unit is backward compatible with an STU-III unit when both units are connected to the PSTN.

The heart of an STE unit is the Fortezza Plus (KOV-14) Crypto Card, which is a PCMCIA card. It contains both the cryptographic algorithms as well as the key(s) used for encryption. Cryptographic algorithms include BATON, FIREFLY, and SDNS signature algorithm. When the Crypto Card is removed from the STE unit, neither the phone or the card is considered classified. BATON is a block cipher developed by the NSA with a block size of 128 bits and key size of 320 bits. FIREFLY, on the other hand, is a key distribution protocol developed by the NSA. The FIREFLY protocol uses public key cryptography to exchange keys between two participants of a secured call.

Both STU-III and STE are built on technologies that are proprietary, and details of the cryptographic algorithms (BATON and FIREFLY) are classified. Although the secrecy of the algorithms does not make the device less secure, it does limit the usage to within the U.S. government and its allies. Within the Department of Defense, Voice over IP (VoIP) has slowly emerged as an alternative solution to STU-III and STE. The high bandwidth of IP networks makes VoIP attractive because it results in voice quality superior to STU-III and STE. To secure VoIP calls, VoIP phones are connected to classified IP networks (e.g. Secret Internet Protocol Router Network – SIPRNET).

Both allies and adversaries of the United States are interested in STU-III, STE, and other secured voice technologies developed by the NSA. To date, there has not been any reported cryptanalysis on the encryption algorithms used by the STU-III and STE. Any breaks in these algorithms could jeopardize national security.

Information about STU-III is very limited despite the fact that it is out of production. Because of the sensitive nature of the subject, there are few relevant documents available on the Internet. The war on terrorism has caused many U.S. government agencies to remove potentially-sensitive information from their websites. The majority of the information available originates from the manufacturers (e.g. L-3 Communications) of STU-III and STE.

43.4 See also

- SIGSALY

- STU-I

- STU-II

- KY-57

- KG-84

- SCIP

- Secure Terminal Equipment

43.5 References

[1] STU-III Phase Out, L3 Communications

43.6 External links

- STU-III Handbook

- STU-III Description, Technical Specification, Pictures

- Report on VOIP and Secure Communications
- The NAVY INFOSEC WebSite on STU-III and STE

Chapter 44

TACLANE

A **TACLANE** (short for "Tactical FASTLANE" or Tactical Local Area Network Encryption) is a family of Inline Network Encryptors (INE) developed and manufactured by General Dynamics C4 Systems to meet the National Security Agency (NSA) requirements for High Assurance Internet Protocol Encryptor (HAIPE version 4.1 as of Nov 2013).[1]

The TACLANE devices are Type 1, key-agile, In-line Network Encryptors that provide network communications security on Internet Protocol (IP) and Asynchronous Transfer Mode (ATM) networks for the individual user or for enclaves of users at the same security level. They are typically deployed in Department of Defense (DOD) tactical and strategic networks, government agencies and their contractors.

TACLANE may also refer to a new series of products, a mobile desktop solution known as the TACLANE Multibook.[2]

TACLANEs allow users to communicate securely over legacy networks such as the Mobile Subscriber Equipment packet network, Nonsecure Internet Protocol Router Network (NIPRNet), Secret Internet Protocol Router Network (SIPRNet), and emerging ATM networks. TACLANEs provide encryption for IP datagram traffic.[3] ATM traffic and IP datagrams are encapsulated in ATM cells to support a variety of IP, ATM, and mixed network configurations. TACLANEs can be used to overlay a secure Virtual Private Network on top of existing public and/or private network infrastructures.

44.1   References

[1] General Dynamics Network Encryption products page

[2] TACLANE MULTIBOOK

[3] TACLANE (KG-175) at Federation of American Scientists

Chapter 45

Type 1 product

In cryptography, a **Type 1 product** is a device or system certified by the National Security Agency (NSA) for use in cryptographically securing classified U.S. Government information.

Type 1 certification is a rigorous process that includes testing and formal analysis of (among other things) cryptographic security, functional security, tamper resistance, emissions security (EMSEC/TEMPEST), and security of the product manufacturing and distribution process.

For a historically oriented list of NSA encryption products (most of them Type 1), see *NSA encryption systems*. For algorithms that NSA has participated in the development of, see *NSA cryptography*.

Types 1 through 4 are defined in the National Information Assurance Glossary (CNSSI No. 4009) which defines Type 1, Type 2, Type 3, and Type 4 **products** and **keys**.

A Type 1 product is defined as:

> *Classified or controlled cryptographic item endorsed by the NSA for securing classified and sensitive U.S. Government information, when appropriately keyed. The term refers only to products, and not to information, key, services, or controls. Type 1 products contain approved NSA algorithms. They are available to U.S. Government users, their contractors, and federally sponsored non-U.S. Government activities subject to export restrictions in accordance with International Traffic in Arms Regulations.*

45.1 See also

- Type 2 product
- Type 3 product
- Type 4 product
- NSA Suite B Cryptography
- NSA Suite A Cryptography

45.2 External links

- National Information Assurance (IA) Glossary (PDF)

Chapter 46

Type 2 product

In cryptography, **Type 2 products** are unclassified cryptographic equipment, assemblies, or components, endorsed by the National Security Agency (NSA), for use in telecommunications and automated information systems for the protection of national security information.

Note: The term refers only to products, and not to information, key, services, or controls. Type 2 products may not be used for classified information, but contain classified NSA algorithms (e.g. CORDOBA) that distinguish them from products containing unclassified algorithms like DES. Type 2 products are subject to export restrictions in accordance with the International Traffic in Arms Regulations.

46.1   See also

- Type 1 product
- Type 3 product
- Type 4 product
- NSA Suite B Cryptography
- NSA Suite A Cryptography

  Parts of this article have been derived from Federal Standard 1037C and from the National Information Systems Security Glossary

Chapter 47

Type 3 product

In NSA terminology, a **Type 3 product** is a device for use with Sensitive, But Unclassified (SBU) information on non-national security systems. Approved algorithms include DES, Triple DES, and AES (although AES might also be usable in NSA-certified Type 1 products).

47.1 See also

- Type 1 product
- Type 2 product
- Type 4 product
- NSA Suite B Cryptography
- NSA Suite A Cryptography

Chapter 48

Type 4 product

In NSA terminology, a **Type 4 algorithm** is an encryption algorithm that has been registered with NIST but is not a Federal Information Processing Standard (FIPS). Type 4 algorithms may not be used to protect classified information.

Alternatively, some sources use "Type 4" specifically to refer to exportable algorithms — once limited to 40-bit keys — which can be relatively easily broken with even a modest amount of computing power.

48.1   See also

- Type 1 encryption
- Type 2 encryption
- Type 3 encryption
- NSA Suite B Cryptography
- NSA Suite A Cryptography

Chapter 49

U-229

This article is about an electrical connector. For the WW-II U-boat, see German submarine U-229. For the Swedish runestone, see Gällsta Runestones.

The **U-229** is a cable connector currently (as of 2009) used by the U.S. military for audio connections to field radios,

Front panel of KY-57 showing U-229 series fill connector in center.

typically for connecting a handset. There are five-pin and six-pin versions. This type of connector is also used by the National Security Agency to load cryptographic keys into encryption equipment from a fill device.

49.1 External links

- U-229 pin-outs and information

Chapter 50

VINSON

This article is about the encryption devices. For other uses, see Vinson.

VINSON is a family of voice encryption devices used by U.S. and allied military and law enforcement, based on the NSA's classified Suite A SAVILLE encryption algorithm and 16 kbit/s CVSD audio compression. It replaces the Vietnam War-era NESTOR (KY-8/KY-28|28/KY-38|38) family.

These devices provide tactical secure voice on UHF and VHF line of sight (LOS), UHF SATCOM communication and tactical phone systems. These terminals are unclassified Controlled Cryptographic Items (CCI) when unkeyed and classified to the keymat of the key when going secure.

VINSON devices include:

- KY-57
- KY-58
- KY-68
- KY-99a (MINTERM)
- KY-100 (AIRTERM)
- KYV-2
- FASCINATOR

VINSON is embedded into many modern military radios, such as SINCGARS. Many multi-algorithm COMSEC modules are also backwards-compatible with VINSON.

50.1 Text and image sources, contributors, and licenses

50.1.1 Text

- **NSA encryption systems** *Source:* https://en.wikipedia.org/wiki/NSA_encryption_systems?oldid=673237087 *Contributors:* TwoOneTwo, Donreed, Kadin2048, Securiger, DavidCary, Inkling, Snap Davies, Matt Crypto, RevRagnarok, Jcm, Pmsyyz, ArnoldReinhold, Kbh3rd, Sietse Snel, Cmdrjameson, Johnteslade, Knowledge Seeker, Woohookitty, Rjwilmsi, Vegaswikian, JYOuyang, Wavelength, Rocketgoat, Kewp, Nymble, Rwwww, Treesmill, SmackBot, Mmernex, Chris the speller, Yanksox, Glloq, ThreeBlindMice, Cydebot, Sysg0d, CosineKitty, Wa3frp, @pple, SoxBot, Jadtnr1, Strykerhorse, Lightbot, Yobot, 7zandec10%, Hkuykend, Enemenemu, BG19bot, ChrisGualtieri, Bobcolby, Foia req and Anonymous: 38

- **AN/CYZ-10** *Source:* https://en.wikipedia.org/wiki/AN/CYZ-10?oldid=598399973 *Contributors:* Edward, Inkling, Matt Crypto, Grm wnr, Pmsyyz, ArnoldReinhold, Engineer Bob, Dual Freq, A.R., Cydebot, Jeremycec, Rees11, Tmaull, ChipChamp, Robert94704, SoxBot, Yobot, BG19bot and Anonymous: 15

- **AN/CYZ-9** *Source:* https://en.wikipedia.org/wiki/AN/CYZ-9?oldid=572245454 *Contributors:* ArnoldReinhold, Cydebot, R'n'B and BG19bot

- **AN/PYQ-10** *Source:* https://en.wikipedia.org/wiki/AN/PYQ-10?oldid=672536511 *Contributors:* ArnoldReinhold, Kenyon, Noclador, SmackBot, A.R., Cydebot, Fnlayson, Tmaull, Flyer22 Reborn, Robert94704, SoxBot, Dthomsen8, Skluser, Yobot, Nameless23, ClueBot NG, BG19bot and Anonymous: 13

- **ANDVT** *Source:* https://en.wikipedia.org/wiki/ANDVT?oldid=589200875 *Contributors:* ArnoldReinhold, Lightmouse, Yobot, 32RB17 and Anonymous: 4

- **Capstone (cryptography)** *Source:* https://en.wikipedia.org/wiki/Capstone_(cryptography)?oldid=519462316 *Contributors:* The Anome, Phr, Khalad, ArnoldReinhold, Mangojuice, Josh Parris, Stardust8212, Eubot, Dr. Sunglasses, Cydebot, R'n'B, SoxBot, Lightbot and Anonymous: 1

- **Clipper chip** *Source:* https://en.wikipedia.org/wiki/Clipper_chip?oldid=676756090 *Contributors:* William Avery, Zhackwyatt, Anders Feder, Ronz, Tempshill, Thue, Raul654, Decrypt3, Inkling, Matt Crypto, Vsmith, ArnoldReinhold, Ropable, AndrewRH, Sukiari, Yojimb0, Patrick-Fisher, Liface, MZMcBride, RexNL, YurikBot, Shaddack, Mlc, Amigan, Knotnic, Peyna, Rearden9, Some guy, SmackBot, Classicfilms, Verne Equinox, Xaosflux, Betacommand, Dids, Bluebot, Frap, Flyne, Watson Ladd, Loadmaster, Zepheus, Jesse Viviano, Cydebot, Hebrides, Capedia, Tawkerbot4, Ab8uu, Thijs!bot, Fx6893, Gioto, Widefox, Darklilac, JXS, CommonsDelinker, Maurice Carbonaro, Crakkpot, DadaNeem, Andyvphil, Amikake3, Technopat, MCTales, SoxBot, Staticshakedown, Addbot, Ironholds, Torla42, Lightbot, Yobot, AnomieBOT, FrescoBot, Sherenati, Miracle Pen, ButOnMethItIs, Lopifalko, Dewritech, Palosirkka, Rayne117, Slowking4, Tgoodspeed, BG19bot, Thom2729, Jdfuvhijfd., Someone not using his real name, Muhammadusman2323, Toadfart, WikiRobert3, Djweitzner, Niftytom and Anonymous: 48

- **CONDOR secure cell phone** *Source:* https://en.wikipedia.org/wiki/CONDOR_secure_cell_phone?oldid=525834910 *Contributors:* Apoc2400, RJFJR, Moreati, Nate1481, SmackBot, SomeBody, ALR, Jim.henderson, Shoessss, Kiranchandran, Yobot, FrescoBot and Anonymous: 2

- **Controlled Cryptographic Item** *Source:* https://en.wikipedia.org/wiki/Controlled_Cryptographic_Item?oldid=618687182 *Contributors:* Beland, Freakofnurture, ArnoldReinhold, Josh Parris, JdforresterBot, Nlu, Mmernex, CBM, LCMan, Cydebot, JAYMEDINC, Magioladitis, PerryTachett, SoxBot, Yobot, Hkuykend, Erik9bot and Anonymous: 1

- **DRYAD** *Source:* https://en.wikipedia.org/wiki/DRYAD?oldid=546754201 *Contributors:* Inkling, Matt Crypto, ArnoldReinhold, Closeapple, Cmdrjameson, Paullaw, Fche, JdforresterBot, Sacxpert, SmackBot, Bluebot, Saejinn, Cydebot, SoxBot, Yobot, Cerabot~enwiki and Anonymous: 4

- **FASCINATOR** *Source:* https://en.wikipedia.org/wiki/FASCINATOR?oldid=498394763 *Contributors:* Topbanana, ArnoldReinhold, Kenyon, AndrewHowse, Lightmouse, Mastersonb, Yobot, Standardschecker and Anonymous: 2

- **Fill device** *Source:* https://en.wikipedia.org/wiki/Fill_device?oldid=618807691 *Contributors:* The Anome, ArnoldReinhold, TransUtopian, Rwwww, Felix116, Magioladitis, Gwern, Cedmunds1, Peizo, ChrisGualtieri and Anonymous: 9

- **Fishbowl (secure phone)** *Source:* https://en.wikipedia.org/wiki/Fishbowl_(secure_phone)?oldid=663114623 *Contributors:* ArnoldReinhold, Funandtrvl, Dawynn, Tim-mnm, Dewritech, GoingBatty, L.J. Tibbs and Anonymous: 4

- **Fortezza** *Source:* https://en.wikipedia.org/wiki/Fortezza?oldid=687871135 *Contributors:* Akadruid, Inkling, Matt Crypto, Conradrock, Sam Hocevar, ArnoldReinhold, Edward Z. Yang, Markussep, Mrzaius, Mu301, Daderot, BjKa, SmackBot, Mauls, Snori, Cydebot, Doca, Jfromcanada, Sillyfolkboy, Yobot, Reezerf and Anonymous: 11

- **General Dynamics C4 Systems** *Source:* https://en.wikipedia.org/wiki/General_Dynamics_C4_Systems?oldid=617416922 *Contributors:* RussBot, SmackBot, Funandtrvl, Shortride, Curtis~enwiki, 718 Bot, Alvin Seville, Erik9bot, Jswizard, MikeGDC4S, Backendgaming, FactCheckDC and Anonymous: 4

- **High Assurance Internet Protocol Encryptor** *Source:* https://en.wikipedia.org/wiki/High_Assurance_Internet_Protocol_Encryptor?oldid=657867816 *Contributors:* Lrreiche, Matt Crypto, Chowbok, Alexkon, Nabber00, Johnteslade, Kenyon, Rjwilmsi, Jmorgan, Abune, SmackBot, Mmernex, Chris the speller, EncMstr, Dmolavi, Derek R Bullamore, Chugnut, Cydebot, Widefox, Dimawik, AlephGamma, Stubb~enwiki, Maurice Carbonaro, HAIPE, EmmaB115, Gerard66, Lightmouse, Bboorman, DoubleVibro, SoxBot, Pbjason9, Bradleyyard, Djctht, Yobot, 7zandec10%, Hkuykend, FrescoBot, Eadsuk, Garyl2010, ClueBot NG, BattyBot, ChrisGualtieri, BFlippo and Anonymous: 34

- **KG-84** *Source:* https://en.wikipedia.org/wiki/KG-84?oldid=647366416 *Contributors:* Matt Crypto, Bobblewik, MementoVivere, ArnoldReinhold, Elipongo, Davidgothberg, Sleigh, Kenyon, Linas, Mindmatrix, Josh Parris, JdforresterBot, NawlinWiki, Eskimbot, Can't sleep, clown will eat me, Kuru, Cydebot, A.Ou, SoxBot, Addbot, Yobot, Materialscientist, Hkuykend, Molestash, Briancarlton and Anonymous: 9

- **KIK-30** *Source:* https://en.wikipedia.org/wiki/KIK-30?oldid=611079102 *Contributors:* ArnoldReinhold and Neøn

- **KIV-7** *Source:* https://en.wikipedia.org/wiki/KIV-7?oldid=621260033 *Contributors:* ArnoldReinhold, Hawaiian717, SmackBot, Magioladitis, Grumpycraig, AKTigger99645, Lightmouse, De728631, Hkuykend, Khazar2, BFlippo and Anonymous: 2

- **KL-43** *Source:* https://en.wikipedia.org/wiki/KL-43?oldid=655887683 *Contributors:* Matt Crypto, ArnoldReinhold, Davidgothberg, Woohookitty, Cydebot, SoxBot, Yobot, Overjive, ClueBot NG and Anonymous: 7

- **KL-51** *Source:* https://en.wikipedia.org/wiki/KL-51?oldid=661387910 *Contributors:* Kku, ArnoldReinhold, Intgr, Mmernex, Pwjb, Cydebot, SoxBot, Lightbot, LittleWink and Trurl1

- **KL-7** *Source:* https://en.wikipedia.org/wiki/KL-7?oldid=661360024 *Contributors:* Kku, Ed g2s, Securiger, Inkling, Matt Crypto, Sam Hocevar, ArnoldReinhold, Davidgothberg, Captain Seafort, Drdefcom~enwiki, Koavf, XLerate, JdforresterBot, SmackBot, Mmernex, Kjhalliwell, Cydebot, Aldis90, Thijs!bot, Niceguyedc, Sv1xv, SoxBot, Addbot, Lightbot, Drpickem, Yobot, Prari, Full-date unlinking bot, Will Beback Auto, BG19bot, Bruce.logan and Anonymous: 6

- **KOI-18** *Source:* https://en.wikipedia.org/wiki/KOI-18?oldid=495003717 *Contributors:* ArnoldReinhold, Stephane.magnenat, GregorB, Grey-Cat, Cynthia Bennett, Hmains, Cydebot, Mikek999, SoxBot, Lindsay3.14, WackyBoots and Anonymous: 5

- **KOV-14** *Source:* https://en.wikipedia.org/wiki/KOV-14?oldid=333089148 *Contributors:* Inkling, Matt Crypto, ArnoldReinhold, DragonHawk, Cydebot, SoxBot and Erik9bot

- **KOV-21** *Source:* https://en.wikipedia.org/wiki/KOV-21?oldid=263257496 *Contributors:* ArnoldReinhold and Anonymous: 1

- **KSD-64** *Source:* https://en.wikipedia.org/wiki/KSD-64?oldid=579275274 *Contributors:* Edward, Inkling, Matt Crypto, ArnoldReinhold, Kenyon, SmackBot, Mikenewton, Cydebot, Magioladitis, Fidelmoquegua, SoxBot, Addbot, Northamerica1000, Shaq123shaq and Anonymous: 2

- **KSV-21** *Source:* https://en.wikipedia.org/wiki/KSV-21?oldid=620913476 *Contributors:* ArnoldReinhold, DragonHawk, SmackBot, Lightbot, Jmanis2 and Anonymous: 1

- **KW-26** *Source:* https://en.wikipedia.org/wiki/KW-26?oldid=679657797 *Contributors:* The Anome, Securiger, Inkling, Matt Crypto, Beginning, ArnoldReinhold, Davidgothberg, Gaius Cornelius, Snarius, N35w101, Mmernex, Janm67, Kingfish, Cydebot, Arch dude, Wa3frp, Eralehm, Sv1xv, SoxBot, Lightbot, Yobot and Anonymous: 8

- **KW-37** *Source:* https://en.wikipedia.org/wiki/KW-37?oldid=677576341 *Contributors:* PaulinSaudi, Inkling, Matt Crypto, ArnoldReinhold, Davidgothberg, Tms, Tabletop, Rwwww, SmackBot, Mmernex, Kingfish, Cydebot, Medconn, Wa3frp, Cb77305, Sv1xv, SoxBot, Lightbot, Yobot, DrilBot, BG19bot and Anonymous: 7

- **KY-3** *Source:* https://en.wikipedia.org/wiki/KY-3?oldid=496127575 *Contributors:* Quadell, Bumm13, ArnoldReinhold, Davidgothberg, Woohookitty, Misterfixit, Azumanga1, Kjhalliwell, Cydebot, R'n'B, SoxBot, Yobot, Salvio giuliano and Anonymous: 2

- **KY-57** *Source:* https://en.wikipedia.org/wiki/KY-57?oldid=506743981 *Contributors:* Magnus Manske, Ray Van De Walker, Smelialichu, Prefect, Angela, Wfeidt, RedWolf, Inkling, Matt Crypto, Rich Farmbrough, ArnoldReinhold, Davidgothberg, Ketiltrout, Engineer Bob, QEDquid, Cydebot, ABF, SoxBot, Yobot, Hellobog and Anonymous: 1

- **KY-58** *Source:* https://en.wikipedia.org/wiki/KY-58?oldid=482742611 *Contributors:* Matt Crypto, Bobblewik, ArnoldReinhold, Davidgothberg, Brookie, Srleffler, Terrybader, OrphanBot, Roidhun~enwiki, NJA, Cydebot, MER-C, SoxBot and Yobot

- **KY-68** *Source:* https://en.wikipedia.org/wiki/KY-68?oldid=681676785 *Contributors:* Zippy, Matt Crypto, Bobblewik, Antandrus, Davidgothberg, Agamemnon2, SmackBot, Roidhun~enwiki, Cydebot, KING OF THE TROLLS!!!, Lucasbfrbot, SoxBot, Chaosdruid, Yobot, A.amitkumar, AuskalorenWiki and Anonymous: 3

- **KYK-13** *Source:* https://en.wikipedia.org/wiki/KYK-13?oldid=608390910 *Contributors:* The Anome, Pmsyyz, ArnoldReinhold, SmackBot, Kuru, Cydebot, Dloomis, ClueBot, SoxBot, Erik9bot and Anonymous: 3

- **Navajo I** *Source:* https://en.wikipedia.org/wiki/Navajo_I?oldid=482743184 *Contributors:* Matt Crypto, ArnoldReinhold, Davidgothberg, Woohookitty, Tawker, Mmernex, Cydebot, WhoFan, Nnemo, SoxBot and Yobot

- **NSA cryptography** *Source:* https://en.wikipedia.org/wiki/NSA_cryptography?oldid=676523574 *Contributors:* Nealmcb, Diberri, Lrreiche, Inkling, Zumbo, Matt Crypto, ArnoldReinhold, Nickj, Tony Sidaway, Mirror Vax, Welsh, SmackBot, Mmernex, Frap, Noah Salzman, Nicblais, BetacommandBot, Think outside the box, AlephGamma, Edgecution, Athaenara, Thundermaker, Mr. Stradivarius, SoxBot, Gail, Yobot, AnomieBOT, Jeremy-parkurst-junior, Gnuish, Msavla77 and Anonymous: 13

- **Over the Air Rekeying** *Source:* https://en.wikipedia.org/wiki/Over_the_Air_Rekeying?oldid=679534089 *Contributors:* The Anome, ArnoldReinhold, The Chief, QEDquid, Tmaull, BG19bot, Ronin Sensei and Anonymous: 6

- **Secure Communications Interoperability Protocol** *Source:* https://en.wikipedia.org/wiki/Secure_Communications_Interoperability_Protocol?oldid=686003723 *Contributors:* Ronz, Aarchiba, Inkling, Matt Crypto, Bobblewik, TheObtuseAngleOfDoom, Jcm, Pmsyyz, ArnoldReinhold, Kbh3rd, Davidgothberg, Cburnett, Pol098, ApprenticeFan, Wongm, RussBot, Brandon, Terrybader, SmackBot, Mmernex, GBL, Bluebot, DantheCowMan, MartinRe, Cydebot, AntiVandalBot, Widefox, CosineKitty, Jay haines, Dekimasu, Julianbashford, Jim.henderson, SoxBot, WikHead, Keir.tomasso, Lightbot, Yobot, Unsourced, Fpietrosanti, W Nowicki, HamburgerRadio, Velowiki, Liechtensteiner~enwiki, Acer FAMS, Cequica and Anonymous: 24

- **Secure DTD2000 System** *Source:* https://en.wikipedia.org/wiki/Secure_DTD2000_System?oldid=668591853 *Contributors:* Pmsyyz, ArnoldReinhold, F, Gracenotes, Cydebot, Serge Harvey-Gauthier, ClueBot, SoxBot, Thecheesykid and Anonymous: 4

- **SINCGARS** *Source:* https://en.wikipedia.org/wiki/SINCGARS?oldid=685323214 *Contributors:* Mav, JeLuF, Ray Van De Walker, Prefect, Ka9q, Wfeidt, DocWatson42, Axeman, Inkling, Marcika, Matt Crypto, Bobblewik, Rich Farmbrough, ArnoldReinhold, Bender235, Nickj, Giraffedata, Mysdaao, Deathphoenix, Woohookitty, Krash, Smeagol92055, D. F. Schmidt, Silver31u, Engineer Bob, SmackBot, Mmernex, Rolypolyman, A.R., PRRfan, Cydebot, Nabokov, Hcobb, Werdnanoslen, L0b0t, Nyq, R'n'B, Zipzipzip, Fg1ff0rd, Tkfussell, Tmaull, AH-Martin, Ingenieurmt, Tahlglass, SoxBot, MystBot, Addbot, Mabraham1, Jomatstaf, Luckas-bot, Yobot, Lammdawg, AnomieBOT, BG19bot, 220 of Borg, ChrisGualtieri, ChamithN and Anonymous: 39

- **STU-I** *Source:* https://en.wikipedia.org/wiki/STU-I?oldid=686001686 *Contributors:* Bumm13, RevRagnarok, ArnoldReinhold, Davidgothberg, Redvers, Woohookitty, MarkPos, RussBot, SmackBot, Scarletsmith, Cydebot, Widefox, Valerius Tygart, Gridiron Scholar, Jim.henderson, Rosiestep, Excirial, SoxBot, Miami33139, Yobot, Capricorn42 and Anonymous: 2

- **STU-II** *Source:* https://en.wikipedia.org/wiki/STU-II?oldid=595905977 *Contributors:* Matt Crypto, WhiteDragon, Bumm13, RevRagnarok, Pmsyyz, ArnoldReinhold, Davidgothberg, Woohookitty, Apokrif, Scarletsmith, Cydebot, Jim.henderson, Whitebox, Dillard421, SoxBot, Yobot, P2Peter and Anonymous: 4

- **STU-III** *Source:* https://en.wikipedia.org/wiki/STU-III?oldid=686003622 *Contributors:* The Anome, AnthonyQBachler, Securiger, Inkling, Counsell, Matt Crypto, WhiteDragon, Bumm13, RevRagnarok, Pmsyyz, ArnoldReinhold, Davidgothberg, Mpeisenbr, RJFJR, Sleigh, Woohookitty, Apokrif, Tabletop, Jonnabuz, ThomasHarte, Wongm, Elhoim, V Brian Zurita, Terrybader, SmackBot, Kintetsubuffalo, Oli Filth, Oni Ookami Alfador, Scarletsmith, Larquitte, CmdrObot, Cydebot, Thecabinet, J Clear, Widefox, Dimawik, Jim.henderson, Lightmouse, Dillard421, Sgroupace, SoxBot, Addbot, Yobot, AnomieBOT, Hkuykend, D'ohBot, JIK1975, Giancarlosg, Molestash, Kulandru mor and Anonymous: 22

- **TACLANE** *Source:* https://en.wikipedia.org/wiki/TACLANE?oldid=632468883 *Contributors:* Chowbok, Pmsyyz, RobyWayne, RussBot, Dan Austin, SmackBot, Bluebot, Cydebot, WVhybrid, MarshBot, Jj137, FrenchChris, Curtis~enwiki, Sephiroth storm, Frmorrison, SoxBot, AnomieBOT, Raphczirr, ClueBot NG, TheJJJunk, RobertNSage and Anonymous: 15

- **Type 1 product** *Source:* https://en.wikipedia.org/wiki/Type_1_product?oldid=578744178 *Contributors:* Tobias Hoevekamp, Timo Honkasalo, The Anome, Andre Engels, LapoLuchini, Imran, Hephaestos, Julesd, Fredrik, Inkling, Matt Crypto, ArnoldReinhold, NetJohn, Schnell, Nuggetboy, Alexbrennen, SmackBot, Mmernex, Brianhull, Chris the speller, Xionbox, Cydebot, Patrick O'Leary, AlephGamma, Rightfully in First Place, Planetary Chaos, SoxBot, Northamerica1000, RotlinkBot and Anonymous: 7

- **Type 2 product** *Source:* https://en.wikipedia.org/wiki/Type_2_product?oldid=479271601 *Contributors:* Tobias Hoevekamp, Robert Merkel, The Anome, Andre Engels, Imran, Hephaestos, Grendelkhan, Fredrik, Inkling, Matt Crypto, TonyW, ArnoldReinhold, Mirror Vax, Peyna, SmackBot, Mmernex, MichaelBillington, Cydebot, AlephGamma, Gigacephalus, SoxBot, Jim1138, ClueBot NG and Anonymous: 5

- **Type 3 product** *Source:* https://en.wikipedia.org/wiki/Type_3_product?oldid=448778736 *Contributors:* Fredrik, Inkling, Matt Crypto, TheObtuseAngleOfDoom, ArnoldReinhold, Danhash, Brandon, SmackBot, Mmernex, GBL, Cydebot, Hydraton31, AlephGamma, SoxBot and Anonymous: 5

- **Type 4 product** *Source:* https://en.wikipedia.org/wiki/Type_4_product?oldid=576094994 *Contributors:* Jni, Inkling, Matt Crypto, Conrad-Pino, ArnoldReinhold, SmackBot, Mmernex, Cydebot, Hydraton31, AlephGamma, SoxBot and Anonymous: 4

- **U-229** *Source:* https://en.wikipedia.org/wiki/U-229?oldid=564493506 *Contributors:* ArnoldReinhold, Woohookitty, Srleffler, A bit iffy, OrphanBot, Gnome (Bot), Cydebot, SoxBot, Lightbot, Legihatp, ConfusedTaffer and Anonymous: 2

- **VINSON** *Source:* https://en.wikipedia.org/wiki/VINSON?oldid=686215822 *Contributors:* Charles Matthews, Inkling, Matt Crypto, Bobblewik, ArnoldReinhold, Davidgothberg, Wtmitchell, Tufflaw, Bky1701, RussBot, Sneak, Terrybader, SmackBot, Mmernex, Dreadstar, Cydebot, Kuyabribri, LorenzoB, Pan Dan, Schmloof, KylieTastic, Rodhullandemu, SoxBot, Addbot, Luckas-bot, Yobot, SporkBot and Anonymous: 5

50.1.2 Images

- **File:Adonis_26_point_rotors.jpg** *Source:* https://upload.wikimedia.org/wikipedia/commons/8/86/Adonis_26_point_rotors.jpg *License:* CC BY-SA 2.5 *Contributors:* Own work *Original artist:* Mark Pellegrini

- **File:Ambox_important.svg** *Source:* https://upload.wikimedia.org/wikipedia/commons/b/b4/Ambox_important.svg *License:* Public domain *Contributors:* Own work, based off of Image:Ambox scales.svg *Original artist:* Dsmurat (talk · contribs)

- **File:CYZ-10_DTD.jpg** *Source:* https://upload.wikimedia.org/wikipedia/commons/9/94/CYZ-10_DTD.jpg *License:* Public domain *Contributors:* ? *Original artist:* ?

- **File:Commons-logo.svg** *Source:* https://upload.wikimedia.org/wikipedia/en/4/4a/Commons-logo.svg *License:* ? *Contributors:* ? *Original artist:* ?

- **File:Cyberright.png** *Source:* https://upload.wikimedia.org/wikipedia/commons/b/b7/Cyberright.png *License:* Public domain *Contributors:* Electronic Frontier Foundation http://w2.eff.org/Misc/Graphics/ *Original artist:* Wired Magazine

- **File:E-8_crewmembers.JPG** *Source:* https://upload.wikimedia.org/wikipedia/en/3/3c/E-8_crewmembers.JPG *License:* PD *Contributors:* www.af.mil

  Original artist:

  Senior Airman Ricky Best

- **File:Edit-clear.svg** *Source:* https://upload.wikimedia.org/wikipedia/en/f/f2/Edit-clear.svg *License:* Public domain *Contributors:* The *Tango! Desktop Project. Original artist:*

  The people from the Tango! project. And according to the meta-data in the file, specifically: "Andreas Nilsson, and Jakub Steiner (although minimally)."

- **File:Emoji_u1f510.svg** *Source:* https://upload.wikimedia.org/wikipedia/commons/3/35/Emoji_u1f510.svg *License:* Apache License 2.0 *Contributors:* https://code.google.com/p/noto/ *Original artist:* Google

- **File:Encryption_sheet_holder.jpg** *Source:* https://upload.wikimedia.org/wikipedia/commons/f/f7/Encryption_sheet_holder.jpg *License:* CC BY-SA 3.0 *Contributors:* Own work *Original artist:* Leonard J. DeFrancisci

- **File:Exelis_SINCGARS_RT-1439.jpg** *Source:* https://upload.wikimedia.org/wikipedia/commons/9/92/Exelis_SINCGARS_RT-1439.jpg *License:* CC BY-SA 3.0 *Contributors:* The item was photographed in our studio *Original artist:* Tahlglass

- **File:Exelis_SINCGARS_RT-1523B.jpg** *Source:* https://upload.wikimedia.org/wikipedia/commons/9/94/Exelis_SINCGARS_RT-1523B.jpg *License:* CC BY-SA 3.0 *Contributors:* Own work *Original artist:* Tahlglass

- **File:Exelis_SINCGARS_RT-1523C.jpg** *Source:* https://upload.wikimedia.org/wikipedia/commons/f/fe/Exelis_SINCGARS_RT-1523C.jpg *License:* CC BY-SA 3.0 *Contributors:* Own work *Original artist:* Tahlglass

- **File:Exelis_SINCGARS_RT-1523E.jpg** *Source:* https://upload.wikimedia.org/wikipedia/commons/6/67/Exelis_SINCGARS_RT-1523E.jpg *License:* CC BY-SA 3.0 *Contributors:* Own work *Original artist:* Tahlglass

- **File:Exelis_SINCGARS_RT-1523F_with_SideHat®.jpg** *Source:* https://upload.wikimedia.org/wikipedia/commons/7/70/Exelis_SINCGARS_RT-1523F_with_SideHat%C2%AE.jpg *License:* CC BY-SA 3.0 *Contributors:* Own work *Original artist:* Tahlglass

- **File:Exelis_SINCGARS_RT-1523G.jpg** *Source:* https://upload.wikimedia.org/wikipedia/commons/8/8c/Exelis_SINCGARS_RT-1523G.jpg *License:* CC BY-SA 3.0 *Contributors:* Own work *Original artist:* Tahlglass

- **File:Exelis_SINCGARS_in_HMMWV.jpg** *Source:* https://upload.wikimedia.org/wikipedia/commons/8/8f/Exelis_SINCGARS_in_HMMWV.jpg *License:* CC BY-SA 3.0 *Contributors:* Own work *Original artist:* Tahlglass

- **File:Flag_of_the_United_States_National_Security_Agency.svg** *Source:* https://upload.wikimedia.org/wikipedia/commons/5/51/Flag_of_the_United_States_National_Security_Agency.svg *License:* Public domain *Contributors:* This vector image includes elements that have been taken or adapted from this: <a href='//commons.wikimedia.org/wiki/File:National_Security_Agency.svg' class='image'><img alt='National Security Agency.svg' src='https://upload.wikimedia.org/wikipedia/commons/thumb/0/04/National_Security_Agency.svg/20px-National_Security_Agency.svg.png' width='20' height='20' srcset='https://upload.wikimedia.org/wikipedia/commons/thumb/0/04/National_Security_Agency.svg/30px-National_Security_Agency.svg.png 1.5x, https://upload.wikimedia.org/wikipedia/commons/thumb/0/04/National_Security_Agency.svg/40px-National_Security_Agency.svg.png 2x' data-file-width='718' data-file-height='718' /></a> National Security Agency.svg. *Original artist:* Fry1989

- **File:GDC4Slogo.png** *Source:* https://upload.wikimedia.org/wikipedia/en/f/f4/GDC4Slogo.png *License:* Fair use *Contributors:* The logo is from the http://www.gdc4s.com website. *Original artist:* ?

- **File:KG-84.navy.jpg** *Source:* https://upload.wikimedia.org/wikipedia/en/8/88/KG-84.navy.jpg *License:* PD *Contributors:* ? *Original artist:* ?

- **File:KL-51.nsa.jpg** *Source:* https://upload.wikimedia.org/wikipedia/commons/a/a8/KL-51.nsa.jpg *License:* CC-BY-SA-3.0 *Contributors:* ? *Original artist:* ?

- **File:KL-7.afca-museum.jpg** *Source:* https://upload.wikimedia.org/wikipedia/en/a/a3/KL-7.afca-museum.jpg *License:* PD *Contributors:* ? *Original artist:* ?

- **File:KL-7_from_front.jpg** *Source:* https://upload.wikimedia.org/wikipedia/commons/4/49/KL-7_from_front.jpg *License:* Public domain *Contributors:* No machine-readable source provided. Own work assumed (based on copyright claims). *Original artist:* No machine-readable author provided. Matt Crypto assumed (based on copyright claims).

- **File:KOI-18.nsa.jpg** *Source:* https://upload.wikimedia.org/wikipedia/commons/8/81/KOI-18.nsa.jpg *License:* CC-BY-SA-3.0 *Contributors:* ? *Original artist:* ?

- **File:KTV1400D.jpg** *Source:* https://upload.wikimedia.org/wikipedia/commons/0/05/KTV1400D.jpg *License:* Public domain *Contributors:* ? *Original artist:* ?

- **File:KW-37R.jpg** *Source:* https://upload.wikimedia.org/wikipedia/commons/f/fc/KW-37R.jpg *License:* CC BY-SA 4.0 *Contributors:* Own work *Original artist:* Medconn

- **File:KW-37T.jpg** *Source:* https://upload.wikimedia.org/wikipedia/commons/3/3e/KW-37T.jpg *License:* CC BY-SA 4.0 *Contributors:* Own work *Original artist:* Medconn

- **File:KY-68.nsa.jpg** *Source:* https://upload.wikimedia.org/wikipedia/commons/8/8d/KY-68.nsa.jpg *License:* CC-BY-SA-3.0 *Contributors:* ? *Original artist:* ?

- **File:KYK-13.nsa.jpg** *Source:* https://upload.wikimedia.org/wikipedia/commons/a/a6/KYK-13.nsa.jpg *License:* CC-BY-SA-3.0 *Contributors:* ? *Original artist:* ?

- **File:KYK-13_Electronic_Transfer_Device.jpg** *Source:* https://upload.wikimedia.org/wikipedia/commons/8/8e/KYK-13_Electronic_Transfer_Device.jpg *License:* Public domain *Contributors:* ? *Original artist:* ?

- **File:Kl-43.jpg** *Source:* https://upload.wikimedia.org/wikipedia/commons/7/7c/Kl-43.jpg *License:* CC-BY-SA-3.0 *Contributors:* ? *Original artist:* ?

- **File:Kl7_rotor_1.jpg** *Source:* https://upload.wikimedia.org/wikipedia/commons/e/e6/Kl7_rotor_1.jpg *License:* Public domain *Contributors:* ? *Original artist:* ?

- **File:Kl7_rotor_2.jpg** *Source:* https://upload.wikimedia.org/wikipedia/commons/7/7c/Kl7_rotor_2.jpg *License:* Public domain *Contributors:* ? *Original artist:* ?

- **File:Ksd-64.jpg** *Source:* https://upload.wikimedia.org/wikipedia/commons/7/72/Ksd-64.jpg *License:* CC-BY-SA-3.0 *Contributors:* took picture at national cryptologic museum *Original artist:* mike newton

- **File:Kw-26-2.jpg** *Source:* https://upload.wikimedia.org/wikipedia/commons/5/53/Kw-26-2.jpg *License:* Public domain *Contributors:* ? *Original artist:* ?

- **File:Kw-26.jpg** *Source:* https://upload.wikimedia.org/wikipedia/commons/d/d7/Kw-26.jpg *License:* Public domain *Contributors:* ? *Original artist:* ?

- **File:Ky-3.jpg** *Source:* https://upload.wikimedia.org/wikipedia/commons/0/02/Ky-3.jpg *License:* CC-BY-SA-3.0 *Contributors:* took picture at national cryptologic museum *Original artist:* mike newton

- **File:Ky-57.jpg** *Source:* https://upload.wikimedia.org/wikipedia/commons/3/3a/Ky-57.jpg *License:* CC-BY-SA-3.0 *Contributors:* ? *Original artist:* ?

50.1.3 Content license